Beyond
Stateliest
Marble

OTHER BOOKS IN THE LEADERS IN ACTION SERIES

Beyond Stateliest Marble

THE PASSIONATE FEMININITY OF ANNE BRADSTREET

DOUGLAS WILSON

LEADERS IN ACTION
GENERAL EDITOR, GEORGE GRANT

CUMBERLAND HOUSE
NASHVILLE, TENNESSEE

Copyright © 2001 by Douglas Wilson

General Editor: George Grant

Published by Cumberland House Publishing, Inc., 431 Harding Industrial Drive, Nashville, Tennessee 37211.

Cover illustration by Bekah Merkle, taken from the stained-glass image of Anne Bradstreet in her home church in England.

Library of Congress Cataloging-in-Publication Data

Wilson, Douglas, 1953–
    Beyond stateliest marble : the passionate femininity of Anne
    Bradstreet / Douglas Wilson.
        p. cm. — (Leaders in action)
    Includes bibliographical references (p.)
    ISBN-13 978-1-58182-164-2; ISBN-10 1-58182-164-6 (alk. paper)
    1. Bradstreet, Anne, 1612?–1672. 2. Poets, American—Colonial
period, ca. 1600–1775—Biography. 3. Women and literature—
Massachusetts—History—17th century. 4. Massachusetts—History—Colonial period, ca. 1600–1775—Biography. 5. Puritans—
Massachusetts—Biography. I. Title. II. Leaders in action series.
PS712 .W56 2001
811'.1—dc21
    [B]   2001028212

Printed in the United States of America

2 3 4 5 6 7 8 9—10 09 08 07

To my granddaughter Jemima Donne Merkle.
May God bless you with a life in which you are
surrounded by beautiful words.

CONTENTS

Acknowledgments

*M*any thanks to Ron Pitkin at Cumberland House, for being willing to have me back again. George Grant has been a most encouraging editor, and Heather Armstrong has been helpful as well. I am indebted to Joost Nixon for his green-inked marginalia on the manuscript. My dear wife Nancy made many appropriate suggestions, although any uses of the passive voice remaining are entirely my fault. And as a teacher of American Lit who was familiar with Anne Bradstreet's work, Nancy was the first to direct me to this very rewarding subject. She and Anne would have been good friends.

FOREWORD

*W*ithout the least historical warrant, the seventeenth-century Puritans have commonly been portrayed as dull and dour. They have been discriminatorily caricatured as artless and plain. They have been unfairly criticized as close-minded and narrow. Nothing could be further from the truth. The Puritans were a colorful, lively, passionate, artful, and delightful people. They took great relish in life. They reveled in the earthly manifestations of beauty, goodness, and truth.

This is particularly evident in the prose and poetry that Puritans—and those Cavaliers and Covenanters sympathetic with their cause—prolifically produced. Indeed, in those heady days just following the Age of Shakespeare, the Puritans and their cultural kith and kin transformed the character of English literature for the good like virtually no other movement before or since. Consider the contributions of such writers as John Donne (1572–1631), William Drummond (1585–1649), Giles Fletcher (1588–1623), George Wither (1588–1667), William Davenport (1606–1688), Jeremy Taylor (1613–1667), Richard Baxter (1615–1691), John Bunyan (1628–1688), Isaac Watts (1674–1748), and, of course, John Milton (1608–1674). By any standard, they afforded us a weighty inheritance of literary treasures.

Clearly, the religious, political, and social upheavals of the day provided those Puritans, Cavaliers, and Covenanters with much to write about. And so they did, with consummate verve, passion, and creativity. Their remarkable emphasis upon substantive education, sublime erudition, and rhetorical excellence was matched only by their emotional maturity, intellectual honesty, and spiritual integrity. The result was a rich body of literature that has continued to shape English-speaking culture ever since.

In the New World, the greatest exponent of this Puritan literary tradition was Anne Bradstreet. As Douglas Wilson demonstrates in this insightful examination of her life and work, she was an epistemologically self-conscious Puritan through and through. She imbibed from the deep wells of Puritan theology all her life. She shared the peculiar Puritan worldview of her Colonial contemporaries— men like Cotton Mather, Nathaniel Ward, and John Winthrop. She accepted the social, cultural, and political mores of those Puritan stalwarts without hesitation. Indeed, she embraces them with no little gusto.

And it was within that context and out of that milieu that America's first great literary works emerged from her pen. It was as a Puritan woman of unswerving conviction that she produced her richly textured verse.

What *Beyond Stateliest Marble* thus affords us is not only a fascinating glimpse into the life and labors of a gifted poet but also a startling reassessment of the entire Puritan world and its impact upon the destinies of men and nations. In other words, Douglas Wilson has accomplished with this book what every biographer ought to accomplish: He has enlightened for us an entire age and not just a single representation of that age.

It is thus a very welcome addition to his already rich contributions to the Leaders in Action series. Indeed, it is a very welcome addition to the essential annals of Christian moral philosophy and their resplendent literary legacy.

—George Grant

CHRONOLOGY OF ANNE BRADSTREET'S LIFE

1483	Martin Luther born.
1492	Columbus discovers America.
1509	Henry VIII crowned.
1517	Martin Luther nails ninety-five theses to Wittenberg door.
1533	Anne Boleyn gives Henry VIII a daughter, Elizabeth I.
1536	William Tyndale martyred, Calvin publishes *Institutes*.
1545	Council of Trent convenes.
1558	Elizabeth I crowned.
1564	John Calvin dies.
1588	Spanish Armada defeated.
1603	King James I crowned.
1603	Simon Bradstreet born.
1611	King James Bible published.
1612	Anne Dudley (Bradstreet) born to Thomas Dudley and Dorothy York Dudley, probably in Northhampton, England.
1619	Canons of Dort affirm the doctrines of grace.
1619	Thomas Dudley becomes steward of the Earl of Lincoln.
1620	Pilgrims sail on the *Mayflower*.
1625	Charles I crowned.
1628	Anne Dudley marries Simon Bradstreet, a young Cambridge graduate. He also is employed by the Earl of Lincoln.
1630	Dudleys and Bradstreets sail for Massachusetts Bay on the *Arbella*. Once there, they move first from Salem to Boston.

1631	In the spring, they move to Cambridge (then called Newtown).
1635	They move to Ipswich (then called Agawam).
1636	Roger Williams banished from the colony.
1637	Anne Hutchinson banished from the colony.
1638	Sometime between '38 and '44 the Bradstreets move to Andover.
1641	Archbishop Laud imprisoned in the Tower of London.
1642	English Civil War breaks out.
1643	Westminster Assembly is convened, and Parliament accepts the Solemn League and Covenant.
1645	Laud is beheaded.
1646	Westminster Confession is completed.
1647	Rev. John Woodbridge (Anne Bradstreet's brother-in-law) sails for England. He probably has a manuscript of Anne's poems with him, unbeknownst to her.
1649	Charles I beheaded.
1650	Bradstreet's book of poetry published in London. It is entitled *The Tenth Muse Lately Sprung up in America*.
1653	Cromwell proclaimed "Lord Protector."
1660	Charles II crowned.
1662	Great Ejection of ministers.
1672	On September 16, Anne Bradstreet dies.
1685	James II crowned. The killing times for Scots Covenanters.
1688	James II deposed.
1689	William and Mary crowned joint sovereigns.

Beyond
Stateliest
Marble

PART 1
THE LIFE OF
ANNE BRADSTREET

"Madam Ann Bradstreet . . . whose poems, divers times printed, have afforded a grateful entertainment unto the ingenious, and a monument for her memory beyond the stateliest marbles."

Cotton Mather

"That our daughters may be as pillars, sculptered in the palace style." (Ps. 144:12b)

UNDERSTANDING THE TIMES

*T*HE SIXTEENTH century was a tumultuous time, and, for the people who lived throughout it, the very ground shifted under their feet. Some of the most obvious manifestations of this were the settlements established in the New World. Many Puritans had crossed the ocean in order to worship God according to the requirements of the Word of God. Because they were virtually the first to arrive in this new setting, a sparsely inhabited continent invited them to establish a city set on a hill. And this is what they set out to do. Their work had a remarkable impact on both sides of the Atlantic.

But they were living in a new world in other senses as well. A generally medieval view of the world was alive and well just a generation before the great emigration to the colonies. The "new science" was not yet established, and while educated individuals were aware of recent scientific advancements, many were not yet convinced by them. This was very true of many of those who crossed over to New England.

The established civil order was in the midst of birth pangs as well. Charles I had embraced an absolutist view of the English monarchy, and his tyranny set in motion the forces that would bring him into a fatal collision with Parliament, and it would result in his beheading. Cromwell ruled as the Lord Protector, but the monarchy was restored after his death, and Charles II brought a dissolute court back into vogue. He was succeeded by James II, who brought the court into such contempt that he was removed in what became known as the Glorious Revolution of 1688.

On the issues surrounding religion and the public square, the seventeenth century was the first time in millennia when significant writers began to seriously broach the idea of a broad religious "tolerance." The idea seemed harmless enough at the beginning, and those who advocated it, like Roger Williams, have been greatly acclaimed—but our generation has been the witness of just how bloodthirsty tolerance can be.

On the issues surrounding religion and the public square, the seventeenth century was the first time in millennia when significant writers began to seriously broach the idea of a broad religious "tolerance." The idea seemed harmless enough at the beginning, and those who advocated it, like Roger Williams, have been greatly acclaimed—but our generation has been the witness of just how bloodthirsty tolerance can be.

And so Anne Bradstreet, the Puritan poetess, lived in a time of great cultural transitions. She was living in a new world, but she had great and deep sympathies for the old order of the old world. Her poetry reflects these transitions; she lived at a very busy crossroads in human history. In some instances we find her looking ahead at the road that was eventually taken. In other situations we see her looking back at the road that was unhappily abandoned. But whichever direction we find her looking, we will discover her to have been a very wise woman indeed.

Influenced by evolutionary assumptions, we moderns have been trained to assume that all these changes and transitions were for the good. And, indeed, some of them were a good thing, but "progress" is by no means an automatic thing. While we may be thankful for modern medicine (and modern dentistry!), our modern cultural rootlessness does not compare well at all with our fathers' sense of *place* and *identity*.

We should consider these changes in turn. As the Puritans came to America, certain changes were inevitable. It was not possible to build a new "nation" without building a new national identity as well. Though they did not initially think that they were building such a new identity does not alter the necessary outcome of their actions. The character exhibited by intrepid explorers and hardy settlers is a type of character that cannot be content with mere duplication of old forms in a new setting. The old forms were brought over, to be sure, but when they were planted here, the new soil affected them drastically, and a breach with the older culture was inevitable.

In addition, the older view of the world, the older cosmology, was still entrenched in England. Challenges there were, but much institutional resistance had to be overcome. That was not the case here, and the older assumptions quickly fell away.

With regard to the civil crisis in Old England, an interesting pattern developed in America that would continue through to the election of Andrew Jackson in the early nineteenth century. The erosion of the old English (unwritten) constitution was well advanced in the old country. The colonists quickly found themselves guardians of the older order—the real civil revolution was occurring back in England. Because of the tyranny of Charles I and the wicked men associated with him, such as Archbishop Laud, the traditional freedoms of Englishmen were under fierce assault. This led to civil war, the effects of which were felt throughout the seventeenth century and most of the eighteenth. The American conservative stance, seeking to maintain the older English order, continued through to the American War for Independence, which really was not a *revolution* at all in the modern sense of the word. The revolutionary activity was happening in England.

We see this as well in the realm of religious "toleration." The chaos of civil disorder in England brought in a weariness with those who wanted an established church, maintaining a united faith that excluded various Protestant sects. This weariness created an opportunity for those who, like Roger Williams or John Milton, wanted to establish "toleration." When the Puritans left for New England, they shared the assumption with virtually every religious party that there could only be one established church. The debate between them concerned which religious party would control the religious establishment. Presbyterians wanted an established church, as did the Independents and the Anglicans. The Puritans who came to America maintained this conviction, but they soon discovered that there had been a fundamental change back home. This explains how Roger Williams could be excluded from Massachusetts Bay but still have very influential friends back in England.

In the midst of this, we find Anne Bradstreet, an educated and intelligent woman with deep Puritan convictions. She was a woman of refinement, living in a newly established hardscrabble colony. She wrote poetry that reflected an educated knowledge of the established science of the day. She took a great interest in the politics of her time and wrote a dialogue between Old England and New, discussing the political troubles of Mother England. She was the daughter of one of New England's magistrates and was married to another one. The local politics in the colony concerned her directly and immediately.

How she dealt with all these things will teach us a great deal about how wisdom views the world.

UNDERSTANDING THE PURITANS

MISUNDERSTANDING THE Puritans is a popular indoor sport for many amateur historians and not a few professionals. Unfortunately, this distorted view frequently comes out in treatments of Anne Bradstreet's life, even when the writer is seeking to be sympathetic to Anne herself. Not all the misconceptions can be set aside in just a few pages, but the general outline of a revisionist view of the Puritans has to be sketched. This is because Anne Bradstreet was a *representative* figure, but she is frequently presented as a Puritan anomaly. She had such a winsome personality, and, since everyone knows that the Puritans were cranks, she is treated as something of a genetic fluke among the Puritans. You see, she was *nice*.[1]

Much of what we think we know about the Puritans is just simply wrong.* For a representative sampling, let's

* After finishing this book, I encountered a wonderful book that really addresses the Puritans and their poetry with genuine insight. It is Robert Daly's *God's Altar: The World and the Flesh in Puritan Poetry.* See Selected Bibliography.

consider the effects of their theology, their view of alcohol, their take on the arts, and their contribution to law.

Admiring (but patronizing) comments abound in literature about the New England Puritans. "The New England Puritans, *in spite of their orthodox views*, were people of broad intellect."[2] In spite of their orthodoxy, they were highly educated. Why not "*because* of their orthodoxy"? The answer is found in the fact that for moderns, belief in God and a brain do not go well together.

For the modern mind, rebellion is authentic, while submission to God is inauthentic. One writer comments: "Here and there in Anne Bradstreet there can be felt also the strain set up between the essential instinctive emotion and the bonds drawn tight against full expression by elements in the Puritan's way of thought."[3] In other words, her theology was a straitjacket that kept her from realizing her full emotional potential.

The writer goes on to discuss Anne Bradstreet's struggle with trials and submission in her poetry on the death of a child. She starts (in the imagination of this writer) to "flicker toward a passionate rebellion" until a bucket of cold theology dowses her. Far better to "rage, rage against the dying of the light," as a modern poet would do. It fits in better for a generation of whiners. In reality, Anne understood herself, and the battle between flesh and spirit, very well. Like all Christians, she had to strive in her faithfulness to God. She was not a bundle of neuroses; she was a Christian growing in the midst of trials. And she did this self-consciously.

In saying this, it is not possible to understand the New England Puritans without understanding the theology of

John Calvin. The Puritans were Calvinists, and, unfortunately, about the only thing more grievously misunderstood today than Puritanism is Calvinism. The situation is complicated because some Puritans did fit the popular caricature, such as Michael Wigglesworth and his dogtrot verse called "The Day of Doom."

And, of course, New England also had her head cases, and some of them made their mark on posterity. One man, a pastor, was called "Handkerchief Moody." He thought he had sinned greatly and would not appear in public without a handkerchief over his face. He would preach with his back to the congregation, but whenever he would turn around, he looked like Jesse James robbing a train. But these were pathological cases, not representative of the sane and sound Puritans. The problem is that moderns like to think of the morbid cases as examples of "the quintessence of Calvinism." Then, when they discover sane and balanced Puritans, these are treated as the exceptions. This is how Anne Bradstreet is regularly represented.

Another erroneous view of the Puritans is that they were a tight-lipped and abstentious people. The word "puritanical" is really a historical slander in this respect. Moderns hear it and assume a tee-totaling fundamentalism. But life in the colony was quite different. "Every family kept on hand a supply of liquor and wine, and cider was considered a necessity of daily living in the country, where it was served with each meal and also carried into the fields by the workers."[4]

We see that the consumption of alcohol was a routine part of a typical Puritan day. Down in Plymouth

Plantation, Bradford once wrote that their water was wholesome, but not, of course, as wholesome as good beer and wine.[5]

For Anne Bradstreet herself, this was a self-conscious issue, and she was a representative Puritan in this. One of her poems put it this way:

> The vintage now is ripe, the grapes are pressed,
> Whose lively liquor oft is cursed and blest;
> For nought so good, but it may be abused,
> But it's a precious juice when well it's used.[6]

It is also commonly maintained that there was a necessary Puritan hostility to festivals such as Christmas, and this is cast in terms of Grinches stealing Christmases. Actually, much of the Puritan problem with such festivals had to do with how they were celebrated at that time—accompanied by carousing, drunkenness, etc. Anne Bradstreet herself makes a positive statement about Christmas. "Through Christendom with great festivity/Now's held (but guessed) for blest Nativity."[7]

Another area of misunderstanding is that of a presumed hostility toward the arts on the part of the Puritans. "The Puritan character did not warm to the fine arts, and austere living was the aim if not always the achievement of the time."[8]

But on a more insightful note, Piercy comments: "The Puritans who were to sail to America in 1630, with the Dudleys and Bradstreets among their number, were by birth and culture Elizabethans. These American immigrants stepped from the most glorious period of English literature."[9]

This literary influence is seen in the work of Anne Bradstreet. Following and developing a different aesthetic standard is not the same thing as being hostile to aesthetic standards. Since this is a book about a Puritan *poet*, the issue of aesthetic standards will be discussed later at some length.

The question of law is another area where the Puritans are greatly misunderstood. The modern mind has a vision of Massachusetts Bay as haven for wannabe ayatollahs and manufacturers of scarlet letters.

But the biblical balance of law and liberty was carefully pursued in early Massachusetts. Rev. Nathaniel Ward, whom we shall meet later as a friend of the Bradstreets (and their minister around 1634), was commissioned to take various earlier efforts that had been made to draft some laws, and to compile and revise them. This he did, and the result was called "the Body of Liberties." The criminal laws were taken largely from the Mosaic Code, which is enough to make many moderns look at them askance. But we often forget our directions—"as a whole, they were much *milder* than the criminal laws of England at that time."[10] In other words, the introduction of biblical law ameliorated the harshness of the existing law.

Ward, the author of these liberties, is taken by some as the quintessential dour Puritan and by others as the last ember of merry old England in New England. "Nathaniel Ward . . . flashes across our early history like a cock pheasant in the gray November woods."[11] An example of his wit gives a good sampling. "I have only two comforts to live upon; the one is in the perfections of Christ; the other is in the imperfections of Christians."[12] But for another perspective on his character, consider this: "Nathaniel Ward, whose name is almost synonymous with orthodoxy and intolerance . . ."[13]

When we consider all these things, one of the first truths to strike us should be that Puritanism in New England cannot be handled in simplistic fashion. And when we study these people sympathetically and carefully, the results of our study might be surprising. We may discover ourselves liking and respecting them.

ANACHRONISTIC HISTORY

*A*NNE BRADSTREET was the kind of woman who modern feminists would love to claim as their own. She was intelligent. She was educated. She thought for herself. That makes her a feminist, right? "If we judge her by her own work, we must discover that her longer, more public works evidence her piety, filial duty, *feminism*, and interest in and wide reading of history, natural science, and literature."[14]

This is to retro-read feminism back into her life and work. Anne Bradstreet was a committed Puritan woman devoted to her God, and she was a woman who adored her very masculine husband. One of the most marked features of her poetry written for her husband is the passionate and personal aspect of it. But one of the tenets of feminism is that women have some kind of sisterhood, a solidarity in the revolutionary sense. This assumption is simply imposed on Anne Bradstreet, and her devotion to her husband is then questioned on the basis of it.

> *What did the warning of the midwife heretic Anne Hutchinson's fate mean for Anne Bradstreet? To what extent is Bradstreet's marriage poetry an expression of individual feeling, and where does it echo the Puritan ideology of marriage, including married love as the "duty" of every god-fearing couple? Where are the stress-marks of anger, the strains of self-division, in her work?*[15]

Anne Bradstreet simply does not fit into our contemporary categories. She was not a feminist in the modern sense, and neither was she an early ur-feminist. She was an intelligent woman who objected to boorish behavior in men, and she also was averse to unscriptural criticisms of her work. But this must be set in the context of her unswerving commitment to the Scriptures, and her lifelong happy devotion to the masculine—God the Father, Christ the Bridegroom, her earthly father, and her devoted husband. "We may see in this why God was her kind, careful parent, while for many Puritans he seems to have been a God of terror."[16] She objected to carping and gossip because they were unscriptural, not because she might have been anticipating her agreements with Gloria Steinem.

She wrote of those who thought a woman ought to leave the world of *belles lettres* alone:

> *I am obnoxious to each carping tongue*
> *Who says my hand a needle better fits,*

> *A poet's pen all scorn I should thus wrong,*
> *For such despite they cast on female wits:*
> *If what I do prove well, it won't advance,*
> *They'll say it's stol'n, or else it was by chance.*[17]

Anne Bradstreet knew that men who preserve their authority by undervaluing the legitimate achievements of women were not masculine. In fact, they were exhibiting their insecurities, the antithesis of masculinity.

> *Let Greeks be Greeks, and women what they are*
> *Men have precedency and still excel,*
> *It is but vain unjustly to wage war;*
> *Men can do best, and women know it well.*
> *Preeminence in all and each is yours;*
> *Yet grant some small acknowledgment of ours.*[18]

In other words Anne had no problem with masculine initiative and leadership. She objected strongly when men were threatened by a competent woman. Her father and her husband were very strong men, and she gloried in that fact. But these very masculine men encouraged her in her education and poetry, and they were not at all threatened by it. In her view a man who objects to some "small" accomplishment by a woman, simply because it was done by a woman, was not much of a man.

As a faithful Puritan, she knew the order of the world. But she also knew that, occasionally, in unusual circumstances, God could use a Deborah. In a poem about Queen Elizabeth I, she wrote:

She hath wiped off th' aspersion of her sex,
That women wisdom lack to play the rex . . .
Was ever people better ruled than hers?[19]

A little later in the poem, she attacks certain "masculines" who say that women are *void* of reason:

Now say, have women worth? or have they none?
Or had they some, but with our Queen is't gone?
Nay masculines, you have thus taxed us long,
But she, though dead, will vindicate our wrong.
Let such as say our sex is void of reason,
Know 'tis a slander now but once was treason.[20]

We see the need for this kind of thinking in our day as well. Because many have come to see how wrong feminism is, they glibly assume that anything that is "not feminism" must be biblical. Anne Bradstreet knew better than this.

Men must assume the leadership, and they must be secure in their masculinity as they do so. This security will be seen in how they respect and honor their wives and daughters as genuinely gifted to aid them in the work for which they are called. One significant indicator of whether they do this will be seen in the education they provide for their daughters. The masculine and the feminine are given by God to work together, point and counterpoint. Man was created in the image of God, male and female together. This was not egalitarian, but men and women were assumed to have been created to complement one another.

In maintaining this, Anne was not resisting the teaching she had received from the Bible—she was applying it. She was not out of step with the Puritan leaders in New England—she was highly respected and honored by them. John Cotton was her pastor. Cotton Mather wrote glowingly of her accomplishments. Nathaniel Ward praised her. Her father and her husband greatly encouraged her. *These* were not the "carping tongues" of which she wrote.

EARLY LIFE AND EDUCATION

*A*NNE DUDLEY was born in 1612 or 1613 in Northamptonshire, England, to Thomas and Dorothy Dudley. Her father was working as a clerk for a noted attorney. Her mother was a well-born gentlewoman.

The Dudley family was descended from a noble family—the Sutton-Dudleys, an ancient family to which Sir Philip Sidney was proud to belong. In one of her poems Anne Bradstreet notes her kinship with Sidney. She came from a noble family, and she was aware of and pleased with it.

Her father had come to Puritan convictions as a young man, which is why his daughter was brought up in the faith. She had a tender conscience, and her early years in the covenant were a great blessing to her.

> *In my young years, about 6 or 7 as I take it, I began*
> *to make conscience of my ways, and what I knew*
> *was sinful, as lying, disobedience to parents, etc. I*
> *avoided it. If at any time I was overtaken with the like*
> *evils, it was as a great trouble, and I could not be at*
> *rest 'till by prayer I had confessed it unto God.*[21]

Around 1619 Anne's father took a post of steward for the Earl of Lincoln. This meant that the Dudleys had to move to the earl's estate at Sempringham, a busy harbor on the east coast of England and a center for the wool trade about eighteen miles from Boston. Anne's parents were members of one of the finest parish churches in England: Saint Botolph's. John Cotton, one of the great Puritan preachers in an era of great preachers, was not only vicar of Saint Boltolph's, but years later he would become the Bradstreets' pastor in America, in a new Boston.

So Anne grew up among the nobility. Her opportunities for enlightening reading and study were great. She was surrounded by a vigorous Puritan aristocracy and had the opportunity to learn music and manners, along with other perks associated with the aristocracy of the day. When she was around nine, her father (who had responsibility for managing all the earl's affairs) brought in a young assistant to help with the estate. Simon Bradstreet, twenty, was a young man who had just earned his B.A. degree from Cambridge. He had earlier been associated with the household of the earl, but he now began work as Thomas Dudley's assistant.

Previously, while Simon Bradstreet had been at the university, he had served as the tutor/governor for the son of a certain Lord Rich (by his first wife Penelope Devereaux. She was the "Stella" of Sir Philip Sidney's sonnets, and later became quite notorious in her immorality.) Her husband divorced her, and Simon Bradstreet spent some time helping with the young son. When Simon went to work for the household of the Earl of Lincoln, he was a mature and experienced young man. His subsequent work showed that his abilities were evident from the beginning.

A few years later Anne was to comment on the beginnings of a spiritual lethargy. "But as I grew up to be about fourteen or fifteen, I found my heart more carnal, and sitting loose from God, vanity and the follies of youth take hold of me."[22] She was not overtly rebellious, but she had begun to drift. An outsider would probably not have noticed anything, but for the Puritans the spiritual life was one of uncompromising zeal. Anne knew in her soul that she had begun to slacken in her concern for the things of God.

In this circumstance the Lord brought a gracious chastisement. "About sixteen, the Lord laid His hand sore upon me and smote me with the smallpox. When I was in my affliction, I besought the Lord and confessed my pride and vanity, and He was entreated of me and again restored me. But I rendered not to Him according to the benefit received."[23]

The smallpox killed multitudes, and disfigured many others. Anne not only survived, but also appears to have been comparatively unscarred by the disease. She asked God to spare her, and He graciously answered her prayer. When she says that she rendered not according to the blessing, she does not mean rebellion but rather insufficient gratitude. In this, she exhibits a typical Puritan awareness that all our efforts fall short of God's standard, and that we can only be accepted by His grace.

Her development into spiritual adulthood was not completed until after her marriage and after she had moved to America.

> *After a short time I changed my condition and was married, and came into this country, where I found a new world and new manners, at which my heart rose. But after I was convinced it was the way of God, I submitted to it and joined to the church at Boston.*[24]

She says here that her "heart rose." This is the only indication of rebellion against spiritual authority that we find in her writings, and it was apparently a short-lived rebellion. When she was convinced that it was the way of God, she joined herself to the church at Boston.

But what was the "it" against which her heart rose? Her reference to "a new world and new manners" indicates that the source of her heart's rising was not a question of the faith itself but more likely a matter of differences in ecclesiastical practice—set in the context of a young aristocratically trained woman adjusting to life in a rough-and-tumble colony.

The most likely candidate for an "issue" was the New England custom of requiring some sort of testimony of God's converting grace before someone was brought into church membership. This was in contrast to the practice of simply receiving into membership someone who was a member in good standing in another sound church. But whatever the difficulty was, Anne was apparently convinced, and was brought into the church at Boston.

From this time on her growth in grace was steady and continual. Subsequent trials would test her, and questions and doubts would present themselves to her. But she walked throughout the rest of her life as a fruitful Christian.

Marriage

A<small>T THE</small> age of sixteen, Anne Dudley married Simon Bradstreet.

Simon, born at Horbling in 1603, was the son of a dissenting minister in Lincolnshire. That explains why he had been reared as a nonconformist—a Puritan. His father had been one of the first fellows of Immanuel College at Cambridge, a college renowned as a hotbed of Puritanism.

His father's death, when Simon was about fourteen years old, interrupted his grammar school education. But within two or three years he was taken into the household of the Earl of Lincoln, one of the most religious of England's noble families. The steward of this household, as it turns out, was Thomas Dudley, Anne Dudley's father. Still, Anne probably did not catch Simon's eye (yet).

Simon spent the next eight years or so working under Thomas Dudley to help manage the earl's various offices. We may also surmise that he spent a good portion of this time watching his future wife grow up. During this time it was suggested to Simon that he attend Immanuel College at Cambridge, which he did for a year. When Bradstreet returned to the earl's household, Thomas Dudley moved on to Boston (England), and the office of steward was given to Simon. From that new position he managed to get the earl's reluctant permission to move on in order to become the steward for the Countess of Warwick. He was a very capable man and discharged his responsibilities for both households faithfully.[25]

It was during his tenure with the Countess that Simon, in 1628, married Anne Dudley. He was twenty-five, and she was sixteen. While they were still newly-weds, she persuaded him to accompany the Dudleys to New England in 1630. And obviously, all the abilities that were so clearly in evidence before Simon left his native country continued with him in the new world.

The marriage between Anne and Simon was a supremely happy one. She was completely devoted to him, and he consistently treated her with tenderness and a strong provision. Some indication of the nature of their marriage can be seen in her poem entitled "To My Dear and Loving Husband":

> *If ever two were one, then surely we.*
> *If ever man were loved by wife, then thee;*

If ever wife was happy in a man,
Compare with me, ye women, if you can.
I prize thy love more than whole mines of gold
Or all the riches that the East doth hold.
My love is such that rivers cannot quench,
Nor ought but love from thee, give recompence.
Thy love is such I can no way repay,
The heavens reward thee manifold, I pray.
Then while we live, in love let's so persevere
That when we love no more, we may live ever.[26]

Her happiness toward Simon is one of the more striking things about her life. He is her *dear* husband in the title of this poem, as well as in a number of others.

This is not surprising, for Simon Bradstreet cut quite a dashing figure. Governor Bradstreet's portrait shows "an attractive man with long hair and the glow of good living—not a dour ascetic, rather more like a Cavalier than the popular idea of the typical Puritan."[27] He provides us with yet another example of how winsome Puritans could be and how consistently this surprises modern readers.

Anne's devotion to her husband was both passionate and very Christian. That is to say, her erotic devotion to him was bounded by Scripture, and set in the context of a close and warm friendship. In one of her poems, when she is anticipating her possible death in childbirth, she speaks of herself as his dear friend:

How soon, my Dear, death may my steps attend,
How soon't may be thy lot to lose thy friend.[28]

To say that she thought a lot of him would be an understatement:

> *My head, my heart, mine eyes, my life, nay, more,*
> *My joy, my magazine of earthly store.*[29]

Because he was a competent man of affairs, Simon frequently traveled to various towns within the colony. When he was gone from home (and once he even had to go back to England to make an appeal to the king), Anne was disconsolate:

> *As loving hind that (hartless) wants her deer,*
> *Scuds through the woods and fern with hark'ning ear.*[30]

Because the Bible is the Word of God, we should not be surprised when those who build their lives on it, as the Puritans sought to do, discover that their lives come to be ordered properly. One place where this order can be plainly seen is within the covenant of marriage.

The marriage of Anne and Simon Bradstreet was not atypical in this respect. The Puritans recovered the biblical teaching that the marriage bed was to be honored and not just tolerated. They gave themselves to the married state with a strong commitment, and one of their great contributions to our culture was the establishment of the view that romantic and erotic devotion was sustainable within the covenant of marriage.

In discussing this, C. S. Lewis once commented that the exaltation of virginity was a Roman Catholic trait, and "that of marriage, a Protestant trait."[31] Leland Ryken makes the same point very well.[32] The Puritan view of the purpose of marriage was threefold—mutual companionship, protection against sexual temptations, and procreation. The Puritans taught that sexual love within marriage was not only lawful, it was supposed to be exuberant and passionate.

The writings left behind by our Puritan fathers and mothers indicates that this view was not just acknowledged, it was widely practiced. And in this, we find that Anne Bradstreet was a faithful Puritan wife.

Voyage on the *Arbella*

Charles I came to the throne of England in 1625. His wife was Catholic, and he supported the Arminian faction within the Church of England. The king had dismissed Parliament, and in 1626 he tried to raise money illegally by levying a forced loan. This met with stiff resistance throughout the country.

One of the most stalwart leaders in this resistance was the Earl of Lincoln. He, along with five other earls, refused to subscribe. Someone within the earl's household published an abridgement of English statutes for free distribution, showing the unconstitutional nature of the king's action. As a result, the book was suppressed and the Earl of Lincoln was prosecuted in the Star Chamber. He was thrown in the Tower until 1628. The following year, the king dissolved Parliament.

The next year, 1630, saw a strong migration of Puritans to Massachusetts. The *Arbella*, named after Lady Arbella Johnson, one of the most distinguished of the

passengers and traveling with her husband Isaac Johnson, carried the Dudleys and Bradstreets to America.
The Johnsons were the only members of nobility on
board, but, unfortunately, neither of them survived the
first year in Massachusetts. Not much information concerning their lives has survived, beyond the fact that
they were highly esteemed and respected by the rest of
the company.

The *Arbella* set sail with three other ships in a
convoy that put to sea from Southampton on April 8,
1630. John Cotton preached the farewell sermon. (He
was to remain in England for a few more years.) It should
be remembered that many of the Puritans had to justify
their leaving England. Many could see severe problems
coming that would involve the king. Some regarded
those leaving as deserters. Part of Cotton's farewell
address concerned the *lawfulness* of going.[33] He was not
to make this choice himself for three more years, but his
endorsement was important. He was the leading Puritan
minister of the day, and his blessing was a great encouragement.

On the voyage over, "Lady Arbella Johnson and the
gentlewomen aboard dined in the great cabin on the
quarterdeck."[34] Given what we know of the stature of
Thomas Dudley and Simon Bradstreet, and their respective positions in the company, this group of gentlewomen
most certainly included Anne Bradstreet and her mother.
The principal men, which also included Governor
Winthrop, ate in the "round house," a cabin in the stern
above the high quarterdeck.

At the same time, all this would have to be considered an honor of *relative* luxury. The *Arbella* was a three-hundred-fifty-ton vessel.[35] This referred to how much water the ship displaced when it was fully loaded. A good portion of that cargo was a variety of drinks for the passengers. For example, another ship in the convoy (a three-hundred-ton vessel named the *Talbot*) was carrying six tons of water and forty-five tons of beer. So in comparison to some of the other ships that came to America, the *Arbella* was a somewhat larger vessel. (The *Mayflower* was a 244-ton ship.) When compared to modern modes of travel, however, the voyage was still one of grinding hardship. "The *Arbella*, of which no exact description has survived, is believed to have been about one hundred and fifty feet in length, with a hold eighteen to twenty feet deep."[36] This is half the length of a football field. They were at sea for two months, finally arriving on June 12.

The men lived in less-than-attractive quarters. "On the *Arbella*, Governor Winthrop's ship, the male passengers lodged on the gundeck."[37] The common practice was to hang hammocks in whatever location could be arranged.

The cooking of food was also an interesting affair. A layer of bricks created a makeshift fireplace. A frame of wood rested on top of the bricks, containing a layer of sand. The fire, usually made of charcoal, was lit on the sand. "More commonly a hearth of bricks was laid on deck, over which stood an iron tripod from which the kettles hung . . . On the ship *Arbella* . . . the 'cookroom' was near a hatchway opening into the hold."[38] Obviously, the possibility of fire was an omnipresent danger.

The quartermaster of the ship would apportion food to each passenger, and they would usually cook their own food at the common hearth—if weather permitted. Given the nature of the case, food was commonly eaten cold. The kind of food they had was predictable: beef, fish, bread, butter, cheese, and oatmeal. While at sea, beer was the principal drink.

But for all the hardship, the voyage of the *Arbella* was relatively uneventful. There was one stillbirth on the *Arbella*, but the other three ships saw seventeen deaths. Although there was no great crisis, they did have one serious scare involving pirates at the beginning of the voyage. Eight sails were spotted astern. The guns were cleared for action, and material that could easily catch fire was thrown overboard. All the men were given either a musket or a crossbow (!). Once they were ready to defend their ship, they went to pray upon the upper deck. The captain, a man of good courage, stood about, only to discover that the ships were friends. Happy salutes were exchanged, and glory was given to God.

Many of the children became seasick, and so the adults arranged a rope from the steerage to the mainmast. All the children, and some others, lined up on both sides of the rope, and swayed it up and down until they were exercised, distracted, and warm. By this means, Governor Winthrop says, "They soon grew well and merry."[39]

After traveling three thousand miles, they finally made landfall. Most were ready to go ashore, but not everyone. "When Governor Winthrop landed at Salem . . . he supped on a good venison pasty and good beer, while most of those who came with him went ashore on Cape Anne side (now Beverly) and gathered strawberries."[40] Presumably, Anne was among those berry pickers.

Early Settlement Conditions

*T*HERE WERE some settlers in Massachusetts Bay prior to 1630, but the first great wave of immigration began with the arrival of the *Arbella*. One of the first concerns, obviously, was the preparation of shelter, particularly in light of the harsh New England winters. These winters were much rougher than in the old country.

We often assume that the early settlers built log cabins, but we are confusing centuries. The kinds of houses varied widely. "At Concord, Mass., the early settlers dug cellars in the earth, which they spanned with wooden spars and then covered with turf."[41] Winthrop also made mention of some of the poorer settlers living in English wigwams.[42] These wigwams were developed off the Indian model, but they had a fireplace and chimney on one end.

Thomas Dudley wrote to the Countess of Lincoln in March 1631. He related, "Wee have ordered that noe man shall build his chimney with wood nor cover his house with thatch, which was readily assented unto, for that divers houses have been burned since our arrival (the fire always beginning in the wooden chimneys) and some English wigwams which have taken fire in the roofes with thatch or boughs."[43]

This letter to the countess was not just a letter to a friend but also designed as something of a formal report. The Puritans back in England were very interested in the affairs of the colony. He also wrote that most homes had had at least one person die, and some households had many. He said, "The naturall causes seem to bee in the want of warm lodgings, and good dyet to which English-men are habittuated."

The settlers who were better off were able to build clapboard houses. In this category we may put both the Dudleys and the Bradstreets. In the homes, cooking fire-places were often called the "chimney." The kitchen was the center of family life—it was the room where the food was cooked and eaten.[44]

Hot water was always available, produced by hang-ing pots over the constant fires. Hasty pudding—made out of cornmeal mush and milk—was a regular. The diet consisted largely of cornmeal, boiled meat, vegetables, and stews.[45]

Life in the early settlements was comparable to life onboard the ships crossing over—hard. But this did not last very long. The "hardships and crudities of the first years were soon replaced by the usual com-forts of the English home of similar station at the same time."[46]

The migration of talent and industry was such that within just a few years, the standard of living for many settlers was comparable to what it had been in England. Glass was being manufactured in Salem as early as 1639.[47] By 1640, there were about twenty-five thousand people living in the colony.[48]

Incidentally, this also accounts (in part) for the "failure" of the Puritan experiment. People of all sorts were flooding in. By 1675, a generation later, a William Harris wrote from Boston that the New England merchants seemed to be wealthy and that their houses were "as handsomely furnished as most in London."[49] Supporting this, Governor Simon Bradstreet in 1680 wrote, in response to a question, that two or three merchants in the colony were worth sixteen to eighteen thousand pounds apiece, with a number of others a little less wealthy.[50]

When Anne Bradstreet arrived, she was a young woman. "She was eighteen, two years married, out of a civilized and humane background."[51] She had endured hardship to get to New England, but she belonged to a family that would do very well. "Her husband was a Cambridge man, a Nonconformist minister's son. Her father, her husband, each was to serve as Governor of Massachusetts; she came to the wilderness as a woman of rank."[52]

The Bradstreets did not pick a place and settle there permanently. Although they first resided near Boston, in 1633 Governor Winthrop had heard that the French were pushing their settlements along the coast, with "divers priests and Jesuits." The governor decided to begin planting towns to the north of Boston. His son, John, along with twelve others, moved and founded Agawam (now Ipswich) in 1633. Two years later, the Bradstreets moved there. Some years later, they moved again, this time to Andover.

Being a woman of station did not exempt one from a common hardship of the era—childbirth. Anne became the mother of eight children and was no stranger to the trials of childbed. "Obstetrics at that period was also a jolly pastime, as the doctor and his volunteer assistants were regaled by a special brew known as 'groaning beer' and by freshly baked 'groaning cakes.'"[53]

In addition to this, for a woman who was having any difficulty in childbirth, some of the available remedies were scary. Here is one example—all natural! "Take a Lock of Vergins haire on any Part of ye head, of half the Age of ye Woman in trauill. Cut it very smale to fine Pouder then take twelve Ants Eggs dried in an ouen after ye bread is drawne or other wise make them dry and make them to pouder with the haire, giue this with a quarter of a pint of Red Cows milk or for want of it giue it in strong ale wort."[54]

Pirates were another problem for the first several generations. This was the golden age, if we can call it that, of piracy. A bloody fight occurred in 1689 near Wood's Hole between a pirate sloop and a vessel in pursuit from Boston. After the fight and after a trial, four of the pirates were sentenced to be hanged. Governor Bradstreet, a man of both conviction and mercy, pardoned three of them and left one to die.[55]

All in all, Anne Bradstreet had significant adjustments to make. "She was a Puritan woman whose early life in physical and intellectual luxury was in direct conflict with the primitive life of the New World."[56] At the same time, she was taught and educated well—and she rose to the occasion.

DAUGHTER OF THE GOVERNOR

ANNE BRADSTREET'S father, Thomas Dudley, was a significant figure in the history of the Massachusetts colony. But his stature and his ability were well in evidence long before he came to the New World.

He was born in 1574, the only son of a military man, Captain Roger Dudley, who was killed in the wars. As an orphan, Thomas was taken into the household of the Earl of Northampton, where he grew up understanding the points of proper behavior. He showed an ability in law while he was a clerk to a man named Judge Nichols, and this served him well throughout the course of his life.

But young Thomas also showed military promise, following in the footsteps of his father. When Queen Elizabeth gave an order to raise soldiers for service in France, "the young sparks" of the Northampton area were not willing to enter into service unless a commission were given to Thomas Dudley to be their captain. This was done, and he led them over to the "low countries." They did not see much action, if any, because a peace treaty was soon concluded, and the men returned to England.

When he returned to Northampton, Thomas married Dorothy, a gentlewoman about whom we know little. Cotton Mather tells us that her "extraction and estate were considerable."[57] Thomas Dudley was also of a family that had a noble past. Although we do not know for certain his grandfather's name, it is probable that he was George Dudley, a Roman Catholic adventurer knight.[58] Although George later became a Protestant, the behavior of the Puritan Dudleys in not mentioning him is understandable. But at the same time, there are clear indications that the Dudleys and Bradstreets were aware of their blueblood lineage.

Around the time that Thomas Dudley married, he came under the influence of Puritan preaching. He was so affected by this ministry that he remained a devout and serious Christian for the rest of his life. He became a nonconformist (with regard to the rites of the Church of England), but at the same time he had little use for the "fanaticisms and enthusiasms" common outside the Church in some quarters.

He was soon recommended as a possible steward to the Earl of Lincoln, who had just come into possession of his earldom. The nobleman's grandfather had run the estate into "vast entanglements," and his father had not been able to straighten it out. The grandson was now faced with this mess, and so he employed Thomas Dudley to take care of business, which he soon did. The estate was laboring under debts of nearly twenty thousand pounds—in that day an enormous sum of money. But Dudley was a shrewd manager, and he soon had the financial affairs in order. In addition, Dudley was used to procure a match in marriage for the Earl, bringing him together with the daughter of the Lord Say. In all this, Dudley rapidly made himself an indispensable fellow.

He continued as steward for nine or ten years until he moved to Boston (England) in order to cultivate a more private life. He probably maintained some kind of working relationship with the earl. During this time he came under the ministry of John Cotton, an association that he greatly appreciated. John Cotton was to become one of the great preachers of New England after the Puritans found their way there. But the Earl of Lincoln couldn't do without Dudley, and he soon recruited him to return.

Dudley served the earl again for a short time until persecution against the Puritans caused him to join himself to the company of émigrés headed to New England. He was elected as their deputy-governor, and it was in that capacity that he arrived on our shores.

Early in his time in America, he was chided by Governor Winthrop for fixing his house up too nice—"for bestowing so much cost on wainscotting his house and otherwise adorning it."[59] Dudley answered that it was done for warmth, not vanity, and anyway, the wainscotting was just clapboard nailed to the walls. This might have been the undercurrent of political differences, because a few years later, in 1634, Dudley was elected governor to replace John Winthrop. In subsequent years, after the death of Winthrop, Dudley was elected governor again and again.

He died on July 31, 1653, at the age of seventy-seven. After his death, some poetry was found in his pocket—showing where Anne's interest, if not her gift, originated:

> *Dim eyes, deaf ears, cold stomach shew*
> *My dissolution is in view.*
> *Eleven times seven near lived have I,*
> *And now God calls, I willing die . . .*
> *Farewel, dear wife, children and friends*
> *Hate heresie—make blessed ends.*
> *Bear poverty; live with good men;*
> *So shall we live with joy agen . . .*[60]

Anne Bradstreet had a very high view of her father. She was a careful student of human nature, and she would have had a keen eye for any hypocritical posturing. And so though Thomas Dudley had a loathing for what was called "toleration," this is only a failing in the eyes of modern observers. *She* saw in him a very godly man:

> *"To Her Father With Some Verses"*
>
> *Most truly honoured, and as truly dear,*
> *If worth in me or ought I do appear,*
> *Who can of right better demand the same*
> *Than may your worthy self from whom it came?*
> *The principal might yield a greater sum,*
> *Yet handled ill, amounts but to this crumb;*
> *My stock's so small I know not how to pay,*

My bond remains in force unto this day;
Yet for part payment take this simple mitee,
Where nothing's to be had, kings loose their right.
Such is my debt I may not say forgive,
But as I can, I'll pay it while I live;
Such is my bond, none can discharge but I,
Yet paying is not paid until I die.[61]

Dudley was a highly respected man. His epitaph (in Latin verse) records that he was a well-read historian, a nonpretentious wit, a champion in debate, a faithful soldier, a catholic and Christian man, and a statesman in New England. But something else still needed to be said of him.

Cotton Mather published his great *Magnalia Christi Americana* in 1702, just forty-nine years after Dudley's death. Mather says, "Thomas Dudly[sic] had a daughter (besides other children) to be a crown unto him . . . Madam Ann Bradstreet, the daughter of our Governor Dudly, and the consort of our Governor Bradstreet, whose poems, divers times printed, have afforded a grateful entertainment unto the ingenious, and a monument for her memory beyond the stateliest marbles."[62]

By any reckoning, Thomas Dudley was a great and influential man. But Mather, a near-contemporary, says that his *crown* was his daughter. This is why those biographers who hunt in her writings for some secret sympathy for the likes of Anne Hutchinson and Roger Williams are yelling up the wrong rain spout. In line with her respect for her father, who was unalterably opposed to them, she could have no doctrinal sympathy for them.[63]

One of her longer poems was dedicated to her father with a short poem at the beginning, which concluded:

> *From her that to yourself more duty owes*
> *Than water in the boundless ocean flows.*[64]

And as she wrote after his death, in a memorial:

> *Let malice bite and envy gnaw its fill,*
> *He was my father, and I'll praise him still.*[65]

In praising him, she was not overlooking his faults—she was praising some of those very things which later generations rejected, but which she did not. She praised, of course, his gift to New England:

> *One of thy Founders, him New England know,*
> *Who stayed thy feeble sides when thou wast low,*
> *Who spent his state, his strength and years with care*
> *That after-comers in them might have share.*[66]

But she also praised his *profound* Puritan convictions:

> *Truth's friend thou wert, to errors still a foe,*
> *Which caused apostates to malign so.*
> *Thy love to true religion e'er shall shine;*
> *My father's God, be God of me and mine.*[67]

And what is for many an embarrassment, was for her a point of honor:

> *Within this tomb a patriot lies*
> *That was both pious, just, and wise,*
> *To truth a shield, to right a wall,*
> *To sectaries a whip and maul . . .*[68]

EARLY POETIC WORK

S HORTLY AFTER arriving in New England, Anne Bradstreet began to work seriously on her poetry. Although her early poetry shows flashes of brilliance, for the most part it is pedestrian apprentice work.

She began as an admirer of Du Bartas, "the leading French Calvinist poet."[69] Du Bartas had been translated into English, not only by Sylvester but also by Sir Philip Sidney. It is worth mentioning that modern critics are astounded that *anybody* could appreciate the work of Du Bartas. But in her admiration, Anne Bradstreet was in good company, company that included Milton in his youth, and John Dryden. Rich says that her admiration for Du Bartas was that of "a neophyte bluestocking." This may be the case, but it is also probable that Du Bartas appealed to certain things that have quite disappeared from the modern consciousness.

Bradstreet acknowledged her debt but also kept her distance. She did not want to be in any way guilty of poetic theft.

> *But feared you'ld judge Du Bartas was my friend.*
> *I honour him, but dare not wear his wealth;*
> *My goods are true (though poor), I love no stealth.*[70]

She was humble about her poetry, and she acknowledged that her "goods were poor." At the same time, her gifts were clear enough to warrant improving upon them.

"That early verse of hers, most often pedestrian, abstract, mechanical, rarely becomes elaborately baroque; at its best her style, even in these apprentice pieces, has a plain modesty and directness which owe nothing to Du Bartas."[71]

Her first work had this in common with Du Bartas—it was encyclopedic. Her "Quaternion" was written between 1630 and 1642.[72] This set of poems included a history of the world (four great ages), a discussion of the makeup of man (four humors), and the ages of man (four).

Her phrases are business-like and to the point. And sometimes they are quaint:

> *Whereof the first so ominous I rained,*
> *That Israel's enemies therewith were brained.*[73]

The main thing her early poetry reveals is not so much her poetic gift as it is the depth and breadth of her education. She was widely read and produced the same kind of encyclopedic poetry as did Du Bartas and Sir Walter Raleigh. She was clearly well educated concerning the history of the world and the medical knowledge of the day.

In addition, some writers suggest that some of her passages seem to show an acquaintance with Shakespeare. The case made seems reasonable.[74] Because of the antipathy that Puritans had for the stage, it is not at all likely that she ever saw a production of any of this work. But she had grown up near, and possibly in, a great library. Her acquaintance could have come about through the comparatively innocent means of reading a book. The case is also strong for a good acquaintance with Chaucer.

But even so, despite this being her time of apprenticeship, she delivers some good lines. In her poem about the humors, one taunt goes home. "Here's sister ruddy, worth the other two."[75] In speaking of mock courage, she speaks tellingly this way: "She loves her sword only because it's gilt."[76]

Her ability to sustain her thoughts in rhymed couplets (her common pattern at this time) was also notable. Writing this way, page after page, is not as easy as it looks:

> *That divine offspring the immortal soul*
> *Though it in all and every part be whole,*
> *Within this stately place of eminence,*
> *Doth doubtless keep its mighty residence.*[77]

Anne also exhibited during this early period a gift for the apt expression. Summer, for example, had "a melted tawny face."[78] She does not attain to the lyric expression she develops later, but an examination of her early work shows us where this gift came from.

LOCAL POLITICAL CONTROVERSIES

*A*S THE daughter of a leading magistrate, and as the wife of another one, Anne Bradstreet had a front-row seat for some of the early controversies in New England. The first great controversy concerned Roger Williams. The second involved Anne Hutchinson.

Anne Bradstreet understood the importance of discipline in the colony. During the turmoil caused by the stubbornness of Roger Williams in 1636—and there was trouble wherever he moved—the political stability of the colony was threatened. Then, during the controversy caused by the heresy of Anne Hutchinson (1637), in which the spiritual health of the colony was under assault, her father was deputy governor of the colony and sat at Hutchinson's trial. Simon Bradstreet was an administrative assistant in the governor's office at the time.[79]

Despite what a number of writers have speculated, Anne Bradstreet would have had no sympathy whatever during these upheavals with the offenders. Everything we know about her militates against this—the only reason that (some secret and unexpressed) sympathy for the troublemakers is routinely attributed to her is that she had such a winsome personality, and everybody knows that Christians who care about heresy *can't* be winsome. But Thomas Hooker called Hutchinson "a pest to the place," and this was a sentiment with which the Bradstreets would have readily agreed.

A few additional words have to said about Roger Williams. Unlike Hutchinson, his name has continued with his legacy, and overwhelmingly he has received good press. Unfortunately, he was, as John Cotton put it, a victim of that "holier than thou" complex that attends so many severe reformers.[80] And there should be no confusion here—Williams was the severe reformer, and the Puritan establishment in New England was the moderate party. Nevertheless, the historical spin that came out of Williams's trial and exile resulted in Williams's achieving some kind of victim status. But this is really out of line with the historical data. In a foreword to a *sympathetic* biography of Williams, Nathan Hatch allowed that he was "a quarrelsome dissenter."[81]

What we have to realize is that Williams was not teaching his doctrines within the confines of his denomination, and that the Puritans, who belonged to another denomination, chased him out of their territory. Williams, a headstrong and obstinate man, taught doctrines that jeopardized the civil integrity of the whole colony. He challenged the right of the king to charter the colony at all (because, Williams maintained, it belonged to the Indians). And at another point, he talked John Endecott into cutting the king's cross out of the colony's flag.

In reality Williams was an obnoxious scrapper. He was far more concerned for "truth" at any cost than were his Puritan opponents. In virtually every respect, and at every stage of the controversy, the Puritans were characterized by a *biblical* charity and Williams was not. But in the eyes of moderns, these personal failings of Williams are excused because of the *content* of his positions—his sympathetic stance toward the Indians, his strong articulation of what he called liberty of conscience, and so forth. He was, we are told, a man ahead of his time. This is quite true—Williams planted seeds that grew up into certain American institutions. Our problem is that we still think of this as a good thing. For example, it is to Williams that we owe the modern notions of separation of church and state. At some points in our history, this was able to masquerade as a good idea, but in our time the secularists have been dismembering infants on the other side of that wall of separation for a generation now, and it is time that we returned to consider some of the first principles that got us here. Many of Williams's Puritan opponents did see where his principles led, and they predicted what would come from it. And here we are, still not having learned.

Anne Bradstreet was not at all deceived by Williams or by Hutchinson. Adrienne Rich notes, "Still, she was devotedly, even passionately married, and through husband and father stood close the vital life of the community . . . Her father was a magistrate at the trial of Anne Hutchinson, the other, heretical, Anne, who threatened the foundations of the colony and 'gloried' in her excommunication."[82]

Anne Hutchinson was an ardent follower of John Cotton, who then took some of his principles out to the end of the road, while neglecting other aspects of his teaching. As a result Cotton initially had a good deal of sympathy for Anne, but as it became clear that she had embraced radically subjective principles concerning the Christian life, Cotton reluctantly had to step aside. This controversy was known in the colony as the "Antinomian" controversy. *Antinomian* means "against the law." The threat posed by her heresy was considerable. She believed herself to be "in direct communication with the God-head, and . . . prepared to follow the promptings of the voice within against all the precepts of the Bible, the churches, reason, or the government of Massachusetts."[83]

She was a capable woman and gathered significant support in the colony, which even included the new governor Henry Vane. She gathered a large following of women in Boston and gave weekly lectures, which, in effect, divided the churches of the colony. She was brought to trial for heresy in 1637 and exiled from the colony in 1638. She came to settle on Long Island, and five years later she and her family were massacred there by a Mohawk attack. In an ironic twist, Roger Williams was sailing for England that same day, and saw the smoke and fire of the attack.[84]

She was, however, a gifted, intelligent woman. And her first name was Anne. But that is where her similarity with Anne Bradstreet ends.

WAR IN OLD ENGLAND

*I*F WE tend to think that the local controversies of New England were complicated, we will stagger when we contemplate the tangle of old England's troubles in the 1640s. And despite the fact that Anne Bradstreet's family was three thousand miles from the strife, they were still, in a very real sense, intimately connected with it.

One of the first things we must keep straight in our minds is that the English Civil War was not a simple affair with two sides neatly divided. Generally, the conflict was between King Charles I and Parliament. But Parliament was also divided between those who might be called "radical Puritans" and those who were much more judicious. Among the judicious Puritans, we may then recognize the Presbyterians and a number of the New England Independents. In England, however, the Independents grew increasingly radical. Although both were opposed to the policies of the king, the Westminster Assembly, a convocation of theologians who produced the Westminster Confession in 1646, was at odds with Parliament. Throw into the mix the fact that Scotland was also a standing threat—with national and ecclesiastical issues jumbled together.

Judicious Puritans are referred to here as those who opposed the king's policies on constitutional grounds yet supported the institution of the monarchy. The watershed issue that helps us maintain this distinction between the radicals and the more judicious is the execution of King Charles I in 1649. Many Puritans were simply appalled at what Cromwell had come to. Anne Bradstreet was in that number.

As she put it:

> *I've seen a king by force thrust from his throne,*
> *And an usurper subtly mount thereon.*[85]

One of the names for Cromwell among the Presbyterian Puritans was "the Destroyer."

Now the migration to New England had been greatly increased because of the persecuting zeal of William Laud, the Archbishop of Canterbury. Charles was forced in 1640 to call what has been called "the Long Parliament." Parliament lost no time in attacking Laud (and his friend Strafford), and in 1641 the Archbishop was imprisoned in the Tower—although he was not beheaded until 1645. (Incidentally, although Laud was a persecutor of the saints and a bigoted man, it must be said that his trial before Parliament was nothing but the preliminary setup prior to a judicial murder.)[86]

The Civil War had broken out into open hostilities in 1642. The Westminster Assembly was convened the following year, and Parliament adopted the Solemn League and Covenant. This covenant declared that the three kingdoms of England, Ireland, and Scotland would each have the same kind of church government, one based on the presbyterian model. In the ensuing tangles, both Charles and Cromwell at different times subscribed to this covenant; and both of them, tragically, became covenant breakers by going back on their word.

During the course of the Civil War, the Rev. John Woodbridge sailed for England. This was in 1647. He was Anne Bradstreet's brother-in-law, married to Anne's sister Mercy. It is likely that he brought Anne Bradstreet's manuscript of poetry with him, with Simon Bradstreet's knowledge and approval.

In the meantime King Charles had been defeated at the Battle of Naseby in 1645. He fled to Scotland in 1646, only to be captured in the north of England in 1647 and taken to Hampton Court. Charles escaped from there and fled to the Isle of Wight. From Carisbrooke Castle, on the Isle of Wight, the king sent word to Parliament that he was willing to discuss terms of peace. Parliament sent commissioners to negotiate with the king. Among them was their chaplain, John Woodbridge, just arrived from New England.

King Charles was executed in 1649, and *The Tenth Muse* was published in London the following year. Elizabeth Wade White argues persuasively in her book that one of the poems in the book was written after the beheading of the king and was an elegy in scriptural disguise. The poem, "David's Lamentation for Saul and Jonathan," would have been sent to Woodbridge or Nathaniel Ward, who were both in England. Anne Bradstreet was a Royalist "by early association in the household of the Earl of Lincoln."[87] She was a staunch Puritan in theology, but she had no use for the radicalism that had commandeered the movement.

White comments that "there were many Puritans who were deeply shocked by the judicial murder of the anointed sovereign but who were obliged, under Cromwell's dictatorship, to hide their feelings or to express them only, as the defeated Royalists did, in veiled and secret ways."[88]

Anne had written a dialogue between Old and New England in 1642 on the eve of the great troubles. Throughout the poem it is evident that she took no delight whatsoever in the escalating turmoil. The indications are that she followed the political events closely and knew who the players were. "Is it Spain? Is it France? Or do the Scots play false behind your back?"[89] But as a true Puritan, she knew exactly what the root cause of the trouble was—idolatry.

> 'Before I tell th' effect, I'll show the cause
> Which are my sins, the breach of sacred laws.
> Idolatry, supplanter of a nation,
> With foolish superstitious adoration . . .
> The Pope had hope to find Rome here again.[90]

Anne Bradstreet knew the political threat that the Roman church still presented and referred to the great slaughter which had occurred in Ireland:

> *Three hundred thousand slaughtered innocents,*
> *By bloody Popish, hellish miscreants.*[91]

At the same time, she knew that civil strife could undo everything and everyone. In the poem, the mother, Old England, warns the daughter colony: "If I decrease, doth think thou shalt survive?"[92] She was not so foolish as to believe that defeat of the king would fix everything. The triumph of Parliament was not, in her understanding, the triumph of right.

TENTH MUSE PUBLISHED

I N 1650 an unpretentious volume appeared in London with quite a pretentious title—in full it was *The Tenth Muse Lately Sprung up in America.*[93]

Publication of the book came as a surprise to Anne, the author, and this resulted in various difficulties. One of them was that Anne, who was fastidious about her work, did not have a chance to contribute to the published work. The book's poems were arranged by Elizabeth White according to the likely date of composition and the consideration of interrelationship of the various poems.

The first of the book's poems was an elegy to Sir Philip Sidney, the great Elizabethan courtier, and relative of the Dudleys. This poem was dated 1638.

She wrote "In Honour of Du Bartas" in 1641. The troubles in England caused her to write "A Dialogue between Old England and New" in 1642 (and which was probably finished in 1643).

Anne wrote a poetic dedication to her father—"To her most Honoured Father Thomas Dudley, Esq." in 1643. This provides the introduction to her encyclopedic poetry. Her poems "The Four Elements" and "The Four Humours" were completed before early 1643. "The Four Ages" and "The Four Seasons" were written between 1643 and 1646.

Her elegy in honor of Queen Elizabeth I was dated in 1643. This is significant, and reveals her royalist sympathies. Civil war had broken out the year before, and Anne turned the subject of her poetry to a time when a strong monarch had reigned.

"The Prologue," "The Four Monarchies," and "Of the Vanity of all Worldly Creatures" were all written (presumably) between 1643 and 1647. The possible lament on the execution of Charles I, "David's Lamentation for Saul and Jonathan" was written (again, possibly) in 1649.

The book was introduced with a number of impressive testimonials, all written in verse. The most significant was that supplied by Nathaniel Ward. The publisher of *The Tenth Muse*, Stephen Bowtell, had three years earlier published a satirical book by Ward called *The Simple Cobbler of Aggawam*. Aggawam was the Indian name for Ipswich, and Ward's persona as a cobbler was thin—he was offering to mend England with his advisory stitches, both in the upper leather and sole. The book was a best-seller in England, and the publisher was probably happy to look at another book recommended by Ward.

Right around the time Ward had made a name for himself with *The Simple Cobbler*, he came back to England, where he was invited to preach before the House of Commons. He preached a vigorous *Puritan* defense of his beloved king, incurring the displeasure of that august assembly. Ward thereafter retired in 1648 to a quiet country parish in Essex, and he died in 1652. During the time of his retirement, Ward wrote his poem commending the poetry of Anne Bradstreet to the world.

In an introductory note, John Woodbridge said, "I feare the displeasure of no person in the publishing these Poems but the Authors, without whose knowledge, and contrary to her expectation, I have presumed to bring to publick view what she resolved should never in such a manner see the Sun."[94] In this, as we shall see, he was at least partially right.

Thomas Dudley, Simon Bradstreet, and John Woodbridge were serious Puritans, and they were doing something in the publishing world that had never been done. Prior to this time there had been an occasional book written by a woman. But nothing like this had ever been done. In this venture, we see a woman of unpretentious rank presuming to handle subject matter of such breadth and depth. These men who brought her into print had a point in what they were doing, and that point, common to conscientious Puritans, was the greater glory of God. They really believed that this work was going to be genuinely edifying to those who bought and read it. They were interested in advancing the kingdom of Christ.

This is interesting because it shows that they had not overreacted to the debacle caused by Anne Hutchinson. They did not maintain that because one woman had veered off into error that all women of parts and substance must therefore keep silent. They did not react; they acted.

Because there were at this time numerous enthusiasts and various fantastic spirits, which drove some women into error, they had to make it plain that Anne Bradstreet was not like this at all. The disclaimers they made are much misunderstood by moderns. Their comments were not patronizing; far from it. Anne was not deserting her station in life; she was *elevating* it.

Again, in the preface, Woodbridge avows that these poems are, in fact, the work of a woman—"honoured, and esteemed where she lives, for her gracious demeanour, her eminent parts, her pious conversation, her courteous disposition, her exact diligence in her place, and discreet managing of her family occasions; and more then so, these Poems are the fruit but of some few hours, curtailed from her sleep and other refreshments."[95]

They were concerned to show that a woman who was godly and educated would elevate the office held by a wife and mother. Put bluntly, a woman can exercise her gifts fully without seeking to compete with men. The feminist error assumes that women can only lead if they do what men do. A traditionalist "masculinism" assumes that a woman's station is inconsistent with any kind of intellectual or cultural attainment.

In the publication of the *The Tenth Muse*, these Puritans were seeking to declare the biblical balance. It would be wrong to say they were ahead of their time. Rather, as we look at the chaos and confusion that afflicts us in the whole matter of sexual roles, it would be better to say that they were ahead of our time.

THE RAMBLING BRAT

S O, THE book was done. Without her knowledge, Anne Bradstreet had become an author. There had been considerable plotting among friends and family to launch the project.[96] When it was finally done, we can only imagine the expression on her face when the book was placed in her hands and how intently her very pleased family watched her. Her emotions, as it turns out, were a combination of embarrassment and gratitude—but, as we shall see, at that moment, she crossed a threshold into artistry.

The Tenth Muse was the only printing under that title (thankfully), and it was the only printing of the book during Anne Bradstreet's lifetime. Although she was embarrassed by various typos and other faults, she accepted the work as her own. One of her reactions was to write the witty poem "The Author to Her Book" in which she calls her book (affectionately) "a rambling brat":

> *Thou ill-formed offspring of my feeble brain,*
> *Who after birth didst by my side remain,*
> *Till snatched from thence by friends, less wise*
>   *than true,*
> *Who thee abroad, exposed to public view,*
> *Made thee in rags, halting to th' press to trudge,*
> *Where errors were not lessened (all may judge) . . .*
> *And take thy way where yet thou art not known;*
> *If for thy father asked, say thou hadst none*
> *And for thy mother, she alas is poor,*
> *Which caused her thus to send thee out of door.*[97]

But another response was far more telling. Anne began the work of revision. The book was hers, and she took responsibility for it. It was published again in 1678, after her death, under the title *Several Poems*. She clearly anticipated this second edition in the editorial work she did, altering some of her earlier poems for this later edition. "For instance, in 'The Four Elements,' lines were added to mention the great fire of London in 1666 and the rebuilding of the city. The account of recent political events in 'Old Age' changed; Cromwell was called a 'Usurper,' a politically wise epithet since the monarchy had been restored."[98]

In addition to this, she continued to write new poems, which were also included in *Several Poems*. These later poems will be discussed in the next chapter; these later poems are by far her best work.

The publication of *The Tenth Muse* revealed Anne Bradstreet's profound humility. She accepted it, and she took pleasure in it. But she did all this without altering the direction and course of her life, and without being distracted by it. Her identity was not that of a poet. She did not adopt poetry as a minor "career." She was a wife and a mother, and she used her poetic gifts from the vantage point of that identity. She did not cling to them as a substitute for that identity. When she later wrote down a prose account of her life for her children, she did not mention her poetry at all. Our tendency is to remember her life in terms of her poetry. When she recalled her life, she did so in terms of her God and her family.

This did not mean that she was apathetic about the book. "Yet neither passing time nor keen self-criticism could banish from her lines to her book, the genuine sense of excitement with which she acknowledged it as her own, and the anxious affection which she made ready to send it forth again 'where yet thou are not known.'"[99]

The publication of this book was a significant milestone. If we do not count the stiff and stilted lyrics of *The Bay Psalm Book* (as we should not), then Anne Bradstreet was the first published American poet. This achievement, considering the circumstances, was remarkable.

From the time of first publication, *The Tenth Muse* showed significant staying power. In 1657 a bookseller in England published an ambitious trade-list of available titles. *The Tenth Muse* is included, indicating good circulation in England seven years after it was initially published. The response to this work was not spectacular, but it has been consistent—for several centuries. Her work was "destined to be reprinted, with the inclusion of Anne Bradstreet's later works, once in its own century and once in the eighteenth, twice in the nineteenth and four times, so far, in our (twentieth) century, so that whoever wished to read Anne's poems could always come upon them, without a great deal of trouble, in a reasonably contemporary edition."[100]

The Tenth Muse was noted critically two times in England in the seventeenth century. A Mrs. Bathsua Makin compiled a list of female poets in antiquity, as well as in foreign countries, and then came to recognize English poets of note. Mrs. Makin was the tutress of the daughter of Charles I, and she was the founder of a school for girls in London. She published her work anonymously in 1673. Part of her design was to argue for the potential excellence of women in poetry. As she put it, "If Women have been good Poets, Men injure them Exceedingly, to account them giddy-headed Gossips, fit only to discourse of their Hens, Ducks, and Geese, and not by any means to be suffered to meddle with Arts and Tongues, lest by intollerable pride they should run mad."[101] In contrast to this, when she begins her English-speaking catalog of women poets, she says this: "How excellent a Poet Mrs. Broadstreet [sic] is (now in America) her works do testify."[102]

Another commentator on the state of poetry in England was Edward Phillips, John Milton's nephew. In 1675 he published *Theatrum Poetarum*. Under a heading of "modern" women who were eminent for poetry, he said this: "Anne Broadstreet, a New-England Poetess, no less in title, viz. before her Poems, printed in Old England anno 1650 . . . the memory of which Poems . . . is not yet wholly extinct."[103]

Three hundred twenty-five years later, we can still say the same thing.

Later Poetic Work

After the publication of *The Tenth Muse,* Anne became a genuine lyric poet. "No more Ages of Man, no more Assyrian monarchs; but poems in response to the simple events of a woman's life: a fit of sickness; her son's departure for England; the arrival of letters from her absent husband; the burning of their Andover house; a child's or grandchild's death; a walk in the woods and fields near the Merrimac River."104

Her early poetry had been decent and noteworthy, but her real literary impact came from the work that would not be published in her lifetime. At the same time, her really fine poetic efforts stood on the shoulders of her apprentice work. If *those* had not been published, then it is not likely that anything else would have been.

Her later work was included in the second edition of her work, *Several Poems.* "The identity of the editor of the 1678 edition has been a mystery, although it was probably no secret in 1678. But someone must have prepared for the press those poems found among the poet's papers after her death, and the most likely person to have done that appears to have been John Rogers, Anne Bradstreet's nephew-in-law, who in 1682 became president of Harvard College."[105] The editor of the second edition clearly had close connections with the family and had worked with the family to include poems found after her death in her papers. John Rogers is the most likely candidate.

With the added poems, Anne Bradstreet finally found her *metier*. Her native voice was familial, lyric, homely, and honest, and it consistently exhibited a plain Puritan loveliness. "'The Author to Her Book' displays a wit quite in keeping with the seventeenth-century, or even Elizabethan, standard."[106]

Of her longer poems, "Contemplations" is her best, with some wonderful turns of phrase—"The trees all richly clad, yet void of pride."[107] In her earlier poetry, the landscapes were flat. What she wrote about nature came more from what she had read about the scenery in Old England than what she had seen in New England. Her descriptions were bookish before, but now it became apparent that she was able to *see* and to translate that into striking images. In this poem, Anne Bradstreet in some ways anticipates the graceful lyricism of the Romantic poets, although her observations were more grounded than theirs, anchored as it was to a biblical orthodoxy:

> *I heard the merry grasshopper then sing.*
> *The black-clad cricket bear a second part;*

> *They kept one tune and play on the same string,*
> *Seeming to glory in their little art.*"[108]

But her lyricism was not limited to nature or the beauties of nature. She had an ability to describe the mundane in such a way as to cause the reader to respond with a shared affection. Her lyrics included her family, her household possessions, her deliverances from illness, and her struggles at the deaths of some of her grandchildren. But beyond every earthly thing, she sang the praises of her husband Simon. Her love and devotion to him at times seems to pass all reasonable bounds— which was exactly how she wanted it.

Sustaining her loves, and her secret of deep contentment in the midst of her griefs, was her thorough knowledge of the sovereignty and authority of God. When the Bradstreet house burned down, she wrote a lovely and deeply touching poem that expresses the trust she had in God in the midst of all His hard providences.

"Calvinism" is often mocked as an austere faith, fit only for ideologues. But in the instructed heart of Anne Bradstreet, and through her pen, we see the loveliness of her Calvinism, which is just a different way of saying the "loveliness of her Christian contentment."

Her grief at the loss of her house, and many of her precious things, is very real. As Calvin himself would say, we are not stocks and stones.

> *Here stood that Trunk, and there that chest;*
> *There lay that store I counted best:*
> *My pleasant things in ashes lye . . .* [109]

But her thoughts do not remain there. As the psalmist frequently does, she reminds herself of what she believes and why. The circumstances do not change, but the eye of faith sees the circumstances in a different light. The decrees of God may be questioned, but never challenged.

> *I blest his Name that gave and took,*
> *That layd my goods now in the dust.*
> *Yea so it was, and so 'twas just.* [110]

By the end of her life, Anne Bradstreet was writing poetry at a high level. She became a poet of significant emotional and lyrical strength. This was not a gift that lightly rested on her, detached from the rest of her life. A careful reading of her poems shows that her loves, her griefs, her shrewdness, her theology, her humor, and her intelligence were all woven together into a consistent whole. She had, in short, a thoroughly Christian worldview, and she lived as she wrote.

She was a genuine minor poet. She does not rank with some of the great poets of surpassing genius—a Dante or a Milton. But at the same time, there has been widespread acknowledgment among informed critics that she was, in truth, a poet in truth.

A WISE WOMAN

ANNE BRADSTREET ended her life "a wise woman in Israel." Her counsel was sought by her adult children, and she was highly respected in the broader community. In this she exemplified how a gifted woman in a biblical community exhibits leadership. She does not do it by pushing ahead of her husband, or by competing with the men. She cultivates wisdom in the station to which God has assigned her, gives herself to the use of her gifts there, and she discovers that her humility comes to be greatly honored.

Nowhere do we find Anne Bradstreet striving for preeminence. She was dutiful, but she did not perform her duties without thought. As an educated, intelligent woman, she employed her gifts in her calling, and discovered that this calling is a profound one. Because of feminist slanders, we moderns are accustomed to saying that someone is "just" a homemaker. Or a woman who is dedicated to her family is often asked if she "works." The implication is that if she is not out in the workforce drawing a paycheck, then she is some kind of a loafer.

Anne gave herself to her husband and children. She was dedicated to the work in front of her. She composed her poetry in the time she carved out of her own hours for rest. While she was living a very full life, she kept her eyes open and considered what was going on around her in the light of what the Bible taught. What she saw and what she learned she recorded.

In addition to her poetry, Anne composed a series of epigrams or meditations at her son Simon's request: "You once desired me to leave something for you in writing that you might look upon, when you should see me no more . . . Such as they are, I bequeath to you; small legacies are accepted by true friends, much more by dutiful children."[111]

With her typical humility, she thought these contributions were a "small" legacy. But to read carefully through these prosaic insights is to see the wisdom and insight of a poetic and biblical thinker. Some of her observations are just what proverbial instruction should consist of—obvious things that almost no one in the target audience sees. "Youth is the time of getting, middle age of improving, and old age of spending; a negligent youth is usually attended by an ignorant middle age, and both by an empty old age."[112] Teenagers think they are bulletproof and don't know that a man reaps what he sows. Someone has to tell them that grass grows up, not down, so that they can know when to roll their eyes.

But children who have been disciplined by real wisdom, and have grown up in it, are eager to be taught—as Anne's children were.

Some of her other meditations show how clearly (and deeply) she understood her Puritan theology, and how well she understood the ease with which men slip off into error when they listen to various carnal whispers.

"Men that have walked very extravagantly and at last bethink themselves of turning to God, the first thing which they eye is how to reform their ways rather than to beg forgiveness for their sins. Nature looks more at a compensation than at a pardon, but he that will not come for mercy without money and without price, but bring his filthy rags to barter for it, shall meet with miserable disappointments, going away empty bearing the reproach of his pride and folly."[113]

If there was one thing that Puritan preachers knew how to do, it was to preach searchingly to the conscience. In Anne's reflections we see how such preaching had a telling effect on those who listened carefully to it over the course of a lifetime. The carnal heart is constantly shying away from *grace* and wants somehow, some way, to earn what it gets.

We also see her wisdom, not only in what she said, but in how much her family wanted her to say it. (I am reminded of my own grandmother at a family reunion, with six mature sons, all hanging on her words and wishes.) The ten commandments require us to honor our father and mother, that our days may go well for us in the land. When parents discipline their children properly when they are little, they continue to honor their parents when they are grown. When they were small, they showed honor through obedience. Once grown, they show honor differently, but they still show it.

Anne Bradstreet was worthy of the honor her family rendered to her. She knew how to touch the point exactly with the needle of wisdom. *Rem acu tetigit.* "Sore labourers have hard hands and old sinners have brawny consciences."[114]

As we read her wisdom and are struck by her understanding, we must recognize, yet again, that Anne was a thoroughgoing Puritan. She cannot be made into something else. Many modern writers are struck with her gracious fruit, and desperately want this to have come from a root other than the one it *did* come from. How could such winsomeness and loveliness come from this gnarled, ugly Calvinistic root? Well, it did.

One biographer, for example, says Anne Bradstreet was trying to "find an outlet for a pent-up rebellion against a new world forced upon her and against the Puritan 'pieties that seemed the weary drizzle of an unremembered dream.'"[115] Right.

Anne Bradstreet was a forgiven sinner, and she knew her struggles and surrenders better than anyone. But she also knew her Savior well, and she had no need for a modern therapist.

PART 2
THE CHARACTER OF ANNE BRADSTREET

LOVE

ANNE BRADSTREET served a God of love, and she reflected His character in many different ways. ". . . the idea of divine and tender love predominates throughout Anne Bradstreet's poems."[1] This observation is quite true, but it has to be rescued from its context, where this particular writer distinguishes this characteristic of Anne's from all those *other* Puritans. "We do not feel that hers was the avenging God of the Puritans."[2]

Those who are familiar with the Bible—as Anne Bradstreet certainly was—know that God is a God of love precisely *because* He has delivered us from the divine wrath that rested upon us. The wrath of God that condemned us because of our sin is what we were delivered *from* in the salvation offered in Christ. This is why the Bible frequently talks about these different aspects of God's character in the same breath. "Therefore consider the goodness and severity of God: on those who fell, severity; but toward you, goodness, if you continue in His goodness. Otherwise you also will be cut off (Rom. 11:22)."

Jesus taught His followers that the person who is forgiven much *loves* much. The source of Christian love is found in the relief and gratitude for deliverance from wrath. Anne Bradstreet typified the Puritan balance at this point. If there is no wrath upon sin, then we are all right entirely on our own—God has not given us that much to be grateful for. And if there is great wrath upon sin and no possibility of forgiveness in sight, then the result is anguish and despair. When both aspects are maintained, the believer knows that the only refuge to be found *from* God is *in* God.

So a balanced understanding of the Christian faith emphasizes both. But, unfortunately, not every reader of history or theology has the same balance. Many modern observers begin with the assumption that love and wrath are utterly inconsistent. They then see that Anne Bradstreet was a loving woman, which she was, and conclude as a result that she didn't really believe in all that wrath stuff. Or they look at a later Puritan, such as Jonathan Edwards, and note that he preached a famous sermon on sinners in the hands of an angry God. They conclude, again falsely, that Jonathan Edwards did not really understand the love of God.

Anne Bradstreet loved her God devotedly. The greatest commandment requires us to love Him, not only with all our hearts, but also with all our minds. This she did, unreservedly. She thought through her faith, studied its doctrines, considered the implications, and loved God as a result.

She did not shrink from how He had revealed Himself. She did not pull back from the difficult questions. And at the center of God's revelation of Himself is the fact that He is a *Father*. One of the central tasks of a Christian is to honor the Father, which she was glad to do (John 5:22–23).

This was no doubt easier for her than for some because she had such a godly model of God the Father in her human father, Thomas Dudley. Some unbelieving scholars like to maintain that the idea of the fatherhood of God is a projection of human fatherhood on to the cosmic screen of heaven. Actually, it is the other way around. "For this reason I bow my knees to the Father of our Lord Jesus Christ, from whom the whole family in heaven and earth is named (Eph. 3:14–15)." The word translated "family" here is *patria*, obviously related to the idea of fatherhood. We do not project fatherhood into the skies; God the Father bestows it upon us. We are, after all, created in His image.

All human fathers are therefore speaking about God the Father in how they bring up their children. Some fathers lie about Him, others tell the truth, and all fall short. But Anne Bradstreet was fortunate to have a father whose integrity and commitment to the Word of God provided her with the security to understand a great deal about what God the Father was like.

And then, blessing upon blessing, she came to a strong marriage with a godly man, Simon.

It has to be said that Anne Bradstreet was a woman who was greatly blessed throughout her life by the men in her life. Among her pastors were John Cotton and Nathaniel Ward, some of the greatest ministers of that day—in a day of great ministers. Her father was a man of great courage and integrity, and her husband rivaled him. Beneath it all was the love of God the Father.

She loved them all, and from that position of responsive love she was able to give love to many others. She was a woman loved, and therefore lovely, and therefore loving.

RESPECT

*T*HE BIBLE nowhere commands wives to love their husbands. It is of course not prohibited, and the general command to all Christians to love their neighbor would certainly include a woman's closest neighbor, her husband. And while Paul tells the older women in the book of Titus to teach the younger women to be "husband-lovers," in context this refers more to the duties of domesticity than it talks about a wife's relationship to her husband.

When wives are exhorted to live in a godly way in their particular station as wives, the duty that is assigned to them is the duty of honoring and respecting their husbands. This is a Christian responsibility at which Anne Bradstreet excelled.

In the book of Ephesians, Paul says, "Nevertheless let each one of you in particular so love his own wife as himself, and let the wife see that she respects her husband (Eph. 5:33)." Peter says something similar. "For in this manner, in former times, the holy women who trusted in God also adorned themselves, being submissive to their own husbands, as Sarah obeyed Abraham, calling him lord, whose daughters you are if you do good and are not afraid with any terror (1 Pet. 3:5–6)."

Anne Bradstreet did not live in a time when Christians were embarrassed by such passages. This was the teaching of the Word of God, and so by definition it had to make good sense. She gave herself to this duty gladly, and we see her respect for her father and her husband come out in her poetry frequently and clearly.

In contrast, in these politically correct days, we are not only embarrassed by what the Bible teaches, we want to shut down any testimony that comes from those ages when this was not the case. But history happened the way it did and not some other way. One of the most irritating characteristics of many modern writers is their inability to keep their current ideological crusades out of their reading (and rewriting) of history. We see Attila the Hun sweeping across Europe, and we want his army to contain more Hispanics. We read about the battle of Marathon and want it to be a victory for the American way. We see a Puritan woman gladly honoring her husband, and we want her to get some therapy for her theological repressions.

But Anne Bradstreet knew how to render a biblical respect. When her father died, her eulogy specified his accomplishments and achievements in detail. Her admiration for her husband is evident. She honored and respected her mother as well. As a good mother, she understood the importance of respecting her sons.

Those who were willing to go to the wilderness of America in order to establish a new civilization are certainly worthy of our respect, and they do have it—in retrospect. But offering this respect costs us very little. We are simply amazed at what they were willing to do. But what did it cost the women who came with their husbands and fathers across the ocean? In other words, *their* respect was translated into very tangible actions.

Thomas Dudley and Simon Bradstreet had to consider the political climate of England and determine, as best they could, what was going to happen to the Puritan cause in that country. They then had to weigh the perils of an ocean crossing, the dangers of establishing themselves in the wilderness, the possibilities of disease and death, and the potential threat from the Indians. Taking all this into account, they had to make a decision—and their women had to trust them. It is a testimony to the strength of their character that their wives unhesitatingly went with them.

Those who render respect set a good example for others, and this helps explain why Anne was herself so well respected—both by her family and by the whole New England colony. Our generation tends to believe that you only get what you demand, and that you have to watch out for your own interests because no one else will do it for you. But the Bible teaches that we gain what we are willing to lose, and that if we grasp at something, it will slip through our fingers. Give, and it shall be given unto you.

Demanding respect is the quickest and most efficient way to lose it. Rendering respect is the biblical way to give, and, in the giving, to receive back what was given in another form. Women who want men to respect them—and there is nothing wrong with desiring this—must learn to render respect. Anne Bradstreet understood this principle very well.

Given her theology of submission, given her humility, given her gracious demeanor, why was Anne Bradstreet not a doormat? Because those who knew her respected her—a woman who embodied respect.

Femininity

*T*HE CLOSE relationship between this chapter and the two that have preceded it should quickly become obvious.

Anne Bradstreet was a woman who was thoroughly secure in her femininity. This security is what makes all attempts to claim her as some kind of an early feminist so ludicrous. As a thoroughly feminine woman, she was oriented to the masculine—not as a competitor but as a helper and complement.

One writer notes, "In her characteristic attitude she worshiped the archetypical male."[3] The apostle Paul teaches that the woman was made for the man and not the other way around (1 Cor. 11:8–9). This hierarchical order was not only something that Anne accepted, it was something in which she gloried. And this, in turn, was her glory, again as Paul assumed it would be (1 Cor. 11:7).

Her life was oriented as a helper to that which was masculine in her life. "Around these three masculine figures most of her loving devotion centered."[4] These three figures referred to here were God the Father, Thomas Dudley, and Simon Bradstreet.

Her devotion to the masculine was the secret of her feminine strength. Women who demand independence of this kind of familial masculinity are like a plant demanding independence from the soil. The effect is to uproot them, bringing in a life of insecurity, propped up here and there by reassurances from a thoughtful therapist and the regulations of some federal agency.

But a woman who is secure in how God has made her, and who rejoices in that position, is set free to grow up into a truly feminine strength. Why would a first-rate woman ever want to be a second-rate man?

According to Anne, women who abandoned their natural strengths were to be censured. In her long poem on the history of the world, she comments on a woman who had disgraced her sex:

> *His wife Semiramis usurped the throne;*
> *She like a brave virago played the rex*
> *And was both shame and glory of her sex.*[5]

At the same time, Anne had no doubts about the *ability* that some women had to rule properly, as can be plainly seen in her encomium to Queen Elizabeth I. In the occasional odd situation, it was right and proper for this to occur, as it once did with Deborah in the Old Testament.

So just as Anne was secure in her femininity, she expected men to be secure in their masculinity. She was happy to acknowledge that men had a better aptitude than she did for certain tasks.

> *My tired brain leaves to some better pen;*
> *This task befits not women like to men.*[6]

But she also expected that turnabout was fair play. Secure men would gladly acknowledge when a woman accomplished something worth noting. The men in her life, grounded Puritans all, had no trouble with this standard. They knew her true femininity and applauded it. And *they* were the ones who established her on the stage of literary history, as a true example of Puritan femininity. They did not tolerate this activity of hers, but rather honored and established it. She wrote the poems, but she did not publish them.

APPROPRIATE LEADERSHIP

*T*HIS BOOK is part of a series on leadership in action. So how is it appropriate to hold up a woman as a leader to be imitated? In unbelieving feminist circles this would be unexceptionable, but among the likely readership of this book, it has probably excited some comment. Is Anne Bradstreet to be considered a leader in the same way that Winston Churchill or Robert E. Lee was? If leadership is exclusively a male preserve, then why a book on Anne Bradstreet?

How is it possible to reconcile what Anne Bradstreet herself believed about her role and calling with the need we have for feminine leaders and examples? Recall again what John Woodbridge said of her. He said *The Tenth Muse* "is the Work of a Woman, honoured and esteemed where she lives, for her gracious demeanor, her eminent parts, her pious conversation, her courteous disposition, her exact diligence in her place, and discreet managing of her Family occasions, and more than so, these Poems are but the fruit of some few houres, curtailed from her sleepe and other refreshments."[7]

Comments like this are antithetical to much that we hear about women today—"exact diligence in her place." We are unlikely to encounter this kind of headline on women's magazines we see at the supermarket: "How you can be a discreet manager of family occasions!" But this domestic place was a place that Anne loved, and so in what sense can we consider her a leader? She was not out in the workplace or running for senate or otherwise competing with men. If we were to set before her what feminine leadership looks like today, she would be appalled.

At the same time, Anne Bradstreet's position as a leader and example is secure because she was married to a leader, and she was the kind of help to him that a competent woman should be. In this way she provides us with a very helpful example of what a biblical and thoroughly feminine leadership looks like.

But in order to understand this, we have to shake loose of some of our modern democratic assumptions. The society of that day was ordered and hierarchical. Further, the column that ran throughout every level of that society consisted of two elements—male and female. A woman who was related to the leaders in that society necessarily had far more influence than a man who occupied a more lowly station. When Bathsheba made a petition to David concerning her son Solomon, she was exercising far more influence than the average stablehand in the royal stables. When Esther interceded on behalf of her people, the Jews, she had far more influence than the average hot dog vendor on the streets of Susa.

Sometimes such leadership by women is exercised completely behind the scenes. In other situations, the woman's position and her views are more public—as we find with Anne Bradstreet. But she was in public view more because of her relationship to leaders. Her poetry was written at home, circulated only at home and among friends, until her husband, father, and others saw what a help it would be to their own work to have it published.

For modern feminists, this is "second-rate" leadership, a mere riding on a husband's coattails. But when the family is seen as an organic whole and egalitarian individualism is rejected, the influence of such women is known throughout society as being profound. Such influence can be used in a godly way, as Bathsheba did, or in a negative way, as Miriam once did, or in a godly response to ungodliness, as Abigail did, or in an evil way, as Lady MacBeth did, to take an example from fiction. But any way it goes, competent, wise women help to direct the destiny of nations.

There are women who chafe under the restrictions, and there are women who glory in them, knowing that God's assignment is perfect, and in no way degrading to them. Jesus taught us that the way up is down, the way to be exalted is to humble yourself. The way to humility is glad acceptance of the station God assigns. When the time and place come for exaltation, He will do it.

When Anne Bradstreet followed her husband to the new world, she had no idea what would come of it. When she quietly wrote poetry for her family in her off hours, she had no idea that she was providing a godly example for many generations of young women—showing them that service to husband and family is a noble calling, that God sees and honors it, and that He is able to use all of a woman's gifts and abilities to His glory as He sees fit. A woman's responsibility is to submit gladly to what the Bible teaches, as she is married to a man who submits gladly to what the Bible teaches.

In doing this, Anne Bradstreet ably fits the pattern that Paul requires in the book of Titus (2:4–5). He says that older women are to instruct (lead) the younger women by urging them to love their husbands and children, and to be discreet, chaste homemakers. And behind this instruction, we can no doubt assume that which undergirds all godly instruction—setting a good example.

FILIAL

*W*E HAVE already noted Anne Bradstreet's devotion to her father. His encouragement of her gifts was a large part of the reason she was able to do what she did. We have to recall how "important his sympathetic interest was to her."[8]

We do not know much about her mother, other than the fact that she came from a well-connected, genteel family. Anne wrote the epitaph when Dorothy Dudley died in 1643, at the age of sixty-one:

> *Here lies,*
> *A worthy matron of unspotted life,*
> *A loving mother and obedient wife . . .*
> *A true instructor of her family,*
> *The which she ordered with dexterity.*[9]

Anne Bradstreet was careful to honor both her father and her mother. And this, not surprisingly, is something the Bible considers important. The Ten Commandments address the point directly:

> *"Honor your father and your mother, that your days may be long upon the land which the Lord your God is giving you (Ex. 20:12)."*

Interestingly, the commandment mentions the "land" that God was giving the ancient Israelites. The New England Puritans very much thought of themselves as heirs of God's covenant promises, and they believed that the blessings and curses set forth in the Old Testament applied to them.

There is some warrant for this in the New Testament, where Paul picks up this commandment to the Jews at Sinai, and applies to the Gentile children in the city of Ephesus—including the promise, which has been expanded. "Children, obey your parents in the Lord, for this is right. 'Honor your father and mother,' which is the first commandment with promise: 'that it may be well with you and you may live long on the earth (Eph. 6:1–3).'"

Apart from these details of interpretation, Anne Bradstreet certainly understood her filial duty to honor both her father and mother. But in doing this, she was not cutting against the grain. Her kind and thoughtful words concerning her mother were not a dutiful saying of some words that had to be said. Everything we know about the Dudleys and Bradstreets indicates considerable closeness—throughout many of their years in New England they lived in the same town, and as neighbors. The families were exceptionally close.

Her words of praise also show what Dorothy valued in common with Anne. Intimidated by feminism, we might cringe at her praise of her mother as an "obedient wife." But note two other comments she makes. Her mother was a "true instructor" of her family, and she "ordered" her household with dexterity.

In the biblical pattern, the wife is the executive of the household. She manages and orders it with diligence. The husband is responsible to provide for the household, to represent the house to the outside world, and to provide spiritual headship and oversight. But in the biblical pattern, the husband does not run the house—his wife does.

This pattern is plainly set before us in Proverbs 31 where the woman whose price is above rubies displays her competent management in about every way that can be imagined. She buys real estate, goes on shopping ventures, she engages in philanthropic activity. She is a wonder.

In fact, this is something which Paul requires in his teaching. "I will therefore that the younger women marry, bear children, *guide the house*, give none occasion to the adversary to speak reproachfully (1 Tim. 5:14)." The word used here for "guide the house" includes the word "despot." The fact that the husband is the spiritual head of his house does not undercut the woman's true authority in the home; rather, it establishes it and is the foundation for it.

So when Anne speaks of her mother as a very capable orderer of her household and the true instructor of her family, she is speaking in biblical categories. These are categories that the Puritans understood very well. The headship of the husband does not mean that the woman is assumed to have no brain and very little to contribute. The biblical view of women is not "barefoot, pregnant, and in the kitchen." The view of the value of a well-run home is much higher than this, and, of course, the view of the one who makes it run well is much higher as well. This is the kind of view which Anne had of her Christian mother.

WIFELY

ANNE BRADSTREET cannot be understood apart from her marriage to Simon. "It is . . . probable that the minister who united the two young Puritans was John Cotton,"[10] and every indication is that he was as good at conducting marriages as he was at preaching.

Over the course of their years together, Anne gave to Simon everything a man could reasonably want from a woman. Because Simon was a young Puritan gentleman, we should expect to find at the center of Simon's desires for a wife the general view of marriage that the Puritans held. And that is exactly what we do find. The Puritans believed that marriage was important for three basic reasons, and each of these can readily be seen in the Bradstreet home.

The first was the idea of companionship and friendship in marriage. In the ancient world, true friendship was assumed to be possible only between men. In the

Roman Catholic tradition, women were regarded more as temptations than friends. But the Puritans exalted the idea of friendship between a man and woman in marriage. Leland Ryken, a scholarly observer of Puritans and their ways, says, "Few ideas unleashed such wellsprings of feeling among the Puritans as their praise of the ideal of the companionate marriage."[11]

Simon and Anne certainly embodied this Puritan commitment to friendship within marriage. They trusted one another, they gave counsel to one another, and they delighted in the company of one another. It distressed them greatly when they had to be apart.

The second aspect of marriage important to the Puritans was erotic devotion. In the modern world we say that men are interested in "sex," but in a Puritan context, the young men were interested in wives who, to put it bluntly, were interested in sex to the glory of God. Their approach to the whole subject was exuberant, and, at the same time, they kept well within the boundaries of decency and propriety. This will be explored in more detail, but here it should be said that Anne was responsive to Simon in a passionate and dedicated way.

And this relates to the third point of marriage, the propagation of children. In Puritan theology, sexual activity was not divorced from its biological function, but neither was it limited to it. They understood sexual activity within marriage as having a threefold function—"procreation, a remedy against sexual sin, and mutual society."[12]

Anne was certainly dedicated to motherhood, that is, with providing Simon with sons and daughters. "She could not have been more than twenty-one years old when Samuel was born, but five or six years of marriage without motherhood had distressed and alarmed her."[13] The Puritans thought in terms of keeping covenant with God over the course of generations. And generations meant the bearing of children, and bringing them up in the life of the covenant.

So not only did she bear Simon children, but she also nurtured and taught them consistently and lovingly. She managed her household well, in much the same way that *her* mother had managed her household. Simon was in the position of the husband in Proverbs 31—he was able to safely trust her with his children and his material goods.

Despite the obstacles Anne had to overcome—the frailty of her health, the fact that she had eight children, the status of the Bradstreet home in the community with its social obligations, life on the colonial frontier, and her turning out an impressive volume of poetry—Simon was able to say that she was an impressive manager of his household. She did him good, and not ill, all the days of their life together.

The Bradstreets were indeed fortunate. They were well suited for one another to begin with, and they were blessed enough to live in an era when men and women were taught their respective duties from the Bible in a thorough and God-honoring way. The end result was the kind of marriage that, unfortunately, is rare today.

At the heart of all her wifely expertise was her friendship with God. And because she was a friend of God, she was able in every way to be a close friend to Simon. The word "friend" in the Bradstreet home was filled with meaning. "In that single familiar word are expressed the trust and pride and devotion of a supremely happy marriage."[14]

LOVELINESS

WE HAVE addressed at some length the loveliness of Anne Bradstreet's character. The Bible teaches us that inner character is the source of all true loveliness. Peter refers to the incorruptible beauty of a gentle and quiet spirit, and shows how holy women adorned themselves for their husbands in this way. In this way Anne Bradstreet was genuinely a lovely woman.

But she was also a *beautiful* woman. In his poetic preface to *The Tenth Muse*, John Woodbridge made this reference to her appearance:

> *There needs no painting to that comely face,*
> *That in its native beauty hath such grace.*

One writer correctly notes, "At the very least, it must be assumed that she had not been permanently marked by the smallpox, for if she had, the lines would be unnecessarily cruel."[15] So we know that she had a native beauty and a comely face. No portrait of her survives, and so this description will have to suffice.

Also, like many other Puritan women, she was glad to adorn herself with lovely clothing. She had a husband who could provide for her, and we know that the Puritans enjoyed dressing in an attractive way in order to honor God.

The common assumption that the Puritans wore funeral clothes year-round as a matter of principle must be challenged. It is fair to say, however, that *some* common fashions were assaulted by *some* of the Puritans, but mostly because lots of *other* Puritans were doing whatever it was. For example, one minister "actually cut off his nephew from his inheritance because he wore his hair long in the prevailing fashion."[16] The key phrase here is "prevailing fashion." The Bradstreets belonged to this "Cavalier" wing of Puritanism. The portraits we have of Simon Bradstreet show him wearing his hair in this prevailing fashion. In other words, we know that the Bradstreets did not subscribe to a dowdy-does-it school of thought.

Another example is the issue of wigs. "Later in the century the offense of wearing long hair was forgotten in the unspeakable sin of wearing wigs."[17] The General Court did condemn the practice of men wearing wigs in 1675. But it would be hard to imagine Cotton Mather as being anything other than the quintessential Puritan, and he looks out at us from his engraving wearing his wig.

So how did Anne probably dress? "As for dress—the women wore bonnets, caps, silk hoods, coifs, forehead cloths, ruffs, and whisks. Gowns, cloaks, mantles, and muffs are mentioned frequently; as are many kinds of lace and even fans and veils."[18]

Nathaniel Ward is frequently cited as an example of Puritan misogyny, but Perry Miller is more accurate and on the mark when he describes Ward as having that "vitality and exuberance" that we call *Elizabethan*.[19] Ward provides a good example of the Bradstreets' social circle. And true, Ward did assault those giddy women who had just enough "squirrel brains" to help them hunt out the latest fashions. Ward is quoted as saying that such women were "the epitome of nothing, fitter to be kicked, if she were of a kickable substance, than either honoured or humored."[20]

But frequently not quoted is what Ward said just before this. His thoughts are worth reproducing: "I honor the woman that can honor herself with her attire; a good text always deserves a fair margin; I am not much offended if I see a trim far trimmer than she that wears it; in a word, whatever Christianity or civility will allow, I can afford with London measure."[21]

This is the position of a strict Puritan. Women who honored themselves in their attire were to be honored, because in this way they honored God and their husbands. In *Worldly Saints*, his wonderful book on the Puritans, Leland Ryken provides a portrait of a Puritan woman dressed in her Sunday clothing, demonstrating that they were "far from indifferent to physical attractiveness."[22]

"Whatever Christianity or civility allows"—and for a Puritan, they allowed for a good deal. And this observation, as mentioned, was from a friend of the Bradstreet family. All the indications are that Anne Bradstreet provided the lovely text, and was supplied by her husband with a fair margin.

PASSIONATE

FROM WHAT we have learned thus far, we can see that the Bradstreets had all the combustible material necessary for a passionate marriage. And this in fact was the case, which is frequently noted by modern observers. "Still, she was devotedly, even passionately married . . ."[23]

But even here, modern confusion about the Puritans and biblical theology unfortunately muddies the water. "Anne Bradstreet's unashamed passion for her adored and adoring husband resulted in a troubled conscience which expressed itself in the poem that S. E. Morison called 'One of the best expressions in English literature of the conflict described by Saint Paul in the eighth chapter of his "Epistle to the Romans"; a conflict that was evidently part of the personal experience of the poetess.'"[24]

Confronted with information like this, one hardly knows where to start responding. But for our purposes, we may note that it was the *seventh* chapter of Romans, not the eighth. And of course Anne did relate to this struggle between flesh and spirit (it *is*, after all, in the Bible). But in Pauline theology the "flesh" is not passion for one's *husband.*

The works of the flesh are plain, Paul taught. They were (and still are) "adultery, fornication, uncleanness, lewdness, idolatry, sorcery, hatred, contentions, jealousies, outbursts of wrath, selfish ambitions, dissensions, heresies, envy, murder, drunkenness, revelries, and the like (Gal. 5:19–21)." People who live this way, Paul said, "will not inherit the kingdom of God (v. 21)." When Anne wrote a poem on the flesh and the spirit, she was writing within biblical (and Pauline) categories, and she understood the text far better than modern critics.

Anne was passionately devoted to Simon and did not have an uneasy conscience about it at all. In stark contrast to the Roman Catholic view, against which the Puritans were reacting, the Puritans had a very high view of marital sex. And this is just what the Bible requires of believers. "Marriage is honorable among all, and the bed undefiled; but fornicators and adulterers God will judge (Heb. 13:4)." The marriage bed is not just to be tolerated, it is to be esteemed and *honored.*

William Gouge, a Puritan writer, taught that man and wife should approach sex "with good will and delight, willingly, readily, and cheerfully."[25] Seaborn Cotton (Anne's son-in-law), when a student at Harvard, copied some passionate Renaissance love poetry into his notebook. Later, when he became a minister, he saw no incongruity in using that same notebook for notes of church meetings.[26] One New England wife complained to her pastor, and then to the congregation, that her husband was neglecting their sex life. The church proceeded to excommunicate the negligent husband.[27] John Cotton called marital abstinence "the dictates of a blind mind."[28]

When it comes to sexual matters, the modern use of the word *puritanical* to describe prudishness is really a very successful historical slander. The Victorians were very prudish, but not the Puritans.

And so we have to understand that Anne Bradstreet was, like many of her contemporaries, erotically mature. In this she was a typical Puritan wife, well instructed on what the Bible teaches and encourages within the confines of marriage. She was further blessed to have a husband whom she respected highly, and who did not place unnecessary obstacles in the way of their sexual happiness.

The Puritans were opposed, of course, to adultery and various other forms of immorality, but not at all to sexual fidelity within the boundaries of a marriage covenant. And they would also have looked askance at a married couple behaving indecently in public. But lawful sex was to be private, not because it was dirty, but rather because it was important to keep from inflaming the sexual desires of others, whose presence would intrude on the privacy of the couple. Sex was to be the private, precious possession of man and wife alone with God.[29]

And this is why we see in Anne's poetry a restrained passion. It was restrained because it was a public expression, but it is not hard to see what lies behind the restraint.

If two be one, as surely thou and I,
How stayest thou there, whilst I at Ipswich lye?[30]

In Puritan thinking, the fact of a sexual relationship between man and wife was public knowledge—it was a public covenant, and to be publicly acknowledged. It was not to be publicly flaunted, but it had to be obvious enough to be *honored*.

In the passion of Anne Bradstreet, we do not see a Puritan anomaly, but rather an intelligent cultivation of a very Puritan virtue.

MATERNAL

WHEN ANNE first married, she did not quickly conceive children. This was a cause of great distress to her, and the occasion, as she put it, of tears and prayers. But the Lord heard her prayers, and she was eventually able to bring eight children into the world. All of them survived to adulthood, which was very unusual in that day, and all but one of them (Dorothy) outlived their mother.

As she brought them up, she treated the distinct personalities of her children with a distinctive wisdom. As she put it, "Diverse children have their different natures: some are like flesh which nothing but salt will keep from putrefaction, some again like tender fruits that are best preserved with sugar. Those parents are wise that can fit their nurture to their nature."[31]

She was a prudent mother, able to anticipate possible accidents. She took this maternal wisdom and in one of her meditations applied it to God's dealings with us. "A prudent mother will not clothe her little child with a long and cumbersome garment; she easily foresees what events it is likely to produce, at the best, but falls and bruises or perhaps somewhat worse. Much more will the allwise God proportion His dispensations according to the stature and strength of the person He bestows them on. Large endowments of honour, wealth, or a healthful body would quite overthrow some weak Christian; therefore God cuts their garments short to keep them in such a trim that they might run the ways of His commandments."[32]

She took solicitous care for her children. In one of her poems (anticipating possible death in childbirth), she asked her husband to select any future wife with the well-being of her children in mind:

> *Look to my little babes, my dear remains.*
> *And if thou love thyself, or loved'st me,*
> *These O protect from step-dames injury.*[33]

In the kindness of God, she had four boys and four girls. Until they left home, the labor and care she took over them was diligent and constant.

> *I had eight birds hatched in one nest,*
> *Four cocks there were, and hens the rest.*
> *I nursed them up with pain and care,*
> *Nor cost, nor labour did I spare,*

Till at the last they felt their wing,
Mounted the trees, and learned to sing.[34]

She knew that they were to be brought up in order to establish lives of their own, and she took this in stride with a wry good humor.

One to the academy flew
To chat among that learned crew.[35]

Her firstborn was Samuel, who graduated from Harvard in 1653.[36] He went on to practice medicine in Boston for many years. His first wife died when he was in the process of moving them to Jamaica. He married again in Jamaica and left behind three children when he died in 1682. These children moved back to Massachusetts to live with their grandfather, Governor Bradstreet.

The second child was Dorothy. She married the son of John Cotton, Rev. Seaborn Cotton—so named because he had been born during a stormy voyage.

Sarah was the third child. She married Richard Hubbard of Ipswich.

Next was a son named Simon, born in 1640. He became a minister and pastored a church in New London, Connecticut. He appears to have had a very close relationship with his mother.

Hannah, number five, married Andrew Wiggins of Exeter, New Hampshire. She died in 1707.

Mercy, number six, married a Nathaniel Wade of Ipswich, who moved later to Medford. We know that there was quite a controversy between Simon Bradstreet and Nathaniel's father about the marriage endowment before the marriage was consummated. The good news is that it was amicably settled at the last.

The seventh was Dudley, born at Andover in 1648. In 1698 he and his family were captured by Indians and held for a short time.

The last child, John, was born in 1652. He lived in Topsfield, which is where he married the daughter of a Rev. William Perkins.

Given the heritage of this household, it is not surprising that the descendants of Simon and Anne included many distinguished citizens. One whose name is probably familiar to most is that of Oliver Wendell Holmes. And much of the downstream distinction can be attributed to the maternal wisdom of Anne Bradstreet.

POETIC

*O*F COURSE, this book has already said a great
deal about the poetry of Anne Bradstreet.
But more needs to be noted about her poetic spirit, and
her position in literary history. She certainly had "an
intellectually active, sensually quick spirit."[37] This is
what might be called a "natural" ingredient. Training
does not put in what God left out. Anne Bradstreet was
born with certain poetic sensitivities.

At the same time, she was trained and educated in
a particular context—"It was within a Puritan aesthetic
that Anne Bradstreet aspired and wrote. What is
remarkable is that so many of her verses satisfy a larger
aesthetic, to the extent of being genuine, delicate
minor poems."[38] Despite the patronizing comment
about the "small" Puritan aesthetic, there is an important point to make here. Many modern critics assume

that any biblical horizons are necessarily small. We must take issue with this, but at the same time we have to grant that the Puritans of New England in the seventeenth century *were* parochial. This is, of course, because everyone is. They were parochial because they were people, not because they were Puritans. Everyone must belong to a *particular* culture. With this qualifier, we can agree that one of the marks of good poetry is that it overflows the boundaries of particular cultures. This is exactly what Anne Bradstreet's lyric poetry does.

Apart from the antipathy to that bogeyman "Puritan dogma," the following comment is insightful: "Anne Bradstreet was the first nondidactic American poet, the first to give an embodiment to American nature, the first in whom personal intention appears to precede Puritan dogma as an impulse to verse. Not that she could be construed as a Romantic writing out of her time. The web of her sensibility stretches almost invisibly within the framework of Puritan literary convention; its texture is essentially both Puritan and feminine."[39]

Given her circumstances, Anne Bradstreet must have been ingrained with a particularly strong poetic impetus. "To have written poems, the first good poems in America, while rearing eight children, lying frequently sick, keeping house at the edge of wilderness, was to have managed a poet's range and extension within confines as severe as any American poet has confronted."[40]

This poetic spirit manifested itself in an unusual place and time. "As for American poetry, except for the Bay Psalm Book, no volume of poetry had been printed

in New England before *The Tenth Muse* was published
in London in 1650."[41]

As a poet, Anne Bradstreet faced in two directions.
We can see her biblical Hebraic roots as she looks to
the past, lamenting Saul and Jonathan:

> *Upon thy places mountainous and high,*
> *How did the mighty fall, and falling die?* [42]

But we can also see in her poetry something of an
anticipation:

> *I once that loved the shady woods so well,*
> *Now thought the rivers did the trees excel.*[43]

The Romantics in the next century divinized nature
along with a sentimental response to nature. In this
regard Anne Bradstreet was totally at odds with them.
She was an orthodox Christian. At the same time, the
Romantics were right in many of the things they
rejected—stiff and dry formalism. In this sense an open-
ness to the creation as it presents itself, declaring the
glory of God, is not only lawful for Christians but also
obligatory.

"In many ways Anne Bradstreet . . . anticipated the
Romantic poets—Wordsworth by over a century and
Thomason by over seventy-five years."[44] In this anticipation she developed a balanced understanding of creation
and sensitive response to it without being thrown head-
long into the Romantic abyss of sentimental autonomy.

Anne turned away from rhyming couplets at just the time that Dryden was perfecting his. And right before the development of the neoclassicism of the eighteenth century, she turned to a genuine, lovely, lyric expression. In other words, she struck a Christian balance and provided the alternative to neoclassicism before there was any, and she sounded the note of sensitive appreciation long before the Romantic overreaction to formalism.

In this she was a true aesthetic leader. She pointed a way that few followed, but she was faithful regardless.

Courage

*T*HE COURAGE of the Puritans was not a passive courage. That is, they were activists—they were not interested in sitting back and "taking it." At the same time, when called upon to suffer for their faith, they were certainly capable of doing so. In the annals of martyrdom, some of the most impressive testimonies to the grace of God operating in the word *courage* can be found among the Puritans.

But their courage was also seen in exploration, on the field of battle, in studying the Word of God, and in taming the wilderness in order to settle there. In all that they did, the Puritans were a people at war. "The Puritan was not at liberty to find true peace or fulfillment in the world; he was a front-line soldier, constantly in action not only against every move of the ancient enemy on the battlefield around him, but also

against the temptations that lurked like insidious traitors in his own breast."[45]

As a people at war, Puritans were constantly on
wartime footing. Anne Bradstreet, along with the others
within her community, faced the perils that confronted
her with simple faith and courage. This courage did not
mean imperviousness to pain but was rather a commitment to persevere for the sake of the truth, regardless of
the pain or danger.

The dangers included, first, the political unrest in
England that in the first place caused the Puritans to seek
a new place in which to live. James I "died in the spring
of 1625, leaving his crown, his notorious favorite the
Duke of Buckingham, and his hatred of the Puritans, to
his handsome, fastidious, and self-willed son."[46] Thus,
when Charles I assumed the throne, the obvious fate of
the Puritans was to continue to be harried out of the kingdom. John Milton once wrote of them—"whom nothing
but the wide ocean, and the savage deserts of America,
could hide and shelter from the fury of the bishops."[47]

When he spoke of the fury of the bishops, he was not
overstating his case for rhetorical effect. The Puritans
knew they were up against a savagery that would not
show mercy to any who wanted to live by the Word of
God. And though the Puritans knew this, they were not
of a breed to mute their criticism of ungodliness in high
places in order to pad their own circumstances. Danger-
ous circumstances often call for the courage of blunt
words. And although Anne was a woman, she followed
all these developments with interest and wrote about
them. "Anne's formal verse reveals an interest in politics,

generally of a controversial kind, that is remarkable for a woman of her time."[48]

But remember here that an "interest in politics" was not the equivalent of watching the Republican National Convention on television. The politics of the day were the prelude to persecution and war, and Anne could at times speak with a toughness that matched the times—as in her reference to "bloudy Popish, hellish miscreants."[49]

The issue of courage was also brought close to home by the consequences of the actions taken by the Puritans to escape the persecutions of those "broad-minded" Anglican bishops. Going to sea was not a trivial matter in that day. There was danger from storms, danger from pirates, and the ever present danger of disease. Disease killed many of the travelers—"consequently a number of the colonists fell ill on the voyage with this dreaded wasting disease [scurvy], and did not long survive their landing in New England."[50]

In that day, as in ours, courage took many different forms. There was courage of conviction, standing against persecutors with an open Bible. There was the courage it took to trust your husband and follow him to a new world. Even conceiving a child was an act of physical courage.

In all of this, we find Anne Bradstreet in her element. Her courage was not brought about by ignorance or insensitivity. Any sincere Christian in such circumstances would find ample opportunities to tremble—as she did. But in case after case, we find her choosing the right thing regardless of the circumstances and regardless of the cost.

Again, C. S. Lewis said that courage is not so much a separate virtue as it is the testing point of all the virtues. Every virtue, every grace, is temporary unless it can withstand an assault that threatens the one who possesses it. And withstanding an assault is not possible apart from simple courage. Cowardice will defend nothing, especially virtue.

Because of this, as we consider Anne Bradstreet's life, we can see how she lived a life, not of quiet desperation, but rather of glad and committed courage.

TENDERNESS

*W*E SOMETIMES have trouble understanding how tenderness and strength can go together. In order to be strong, we harden ourselves in a wrong way, a way which makes tenderness impossible. Or we opt for tenderness, and render ourselves incapable of functioning.

We have already mentioned the poem in which Anne is speaking to her husband before the birth of one of her children. She asks him to remember her in various ways, to remember her virtues, and forget her faults. It is a very tender poem. But "Neither bathos nor self-indulgence cloud the economy of these lines; they are honest, tender, and homely as a letter out of a marriage in which the lovers are also friends."[51]

It is important to note that in composing such a poem before childbirth, she was not being maudlin. A woman preparing for childbirth in those days frequently had the same kind of odds that a man preparing for battle had. In other words, death was common, and in some cases, likely. Her poem is composed on the eve of battle, and she is asking her husband to do what should be done if the Lord takes her life.

Her tenderness here is not the result of fear connected to the consequences of actually dying. Christian grief is the kind of thing one sees at airports when a loved one is going away for a long time, and the anticipation of such grief works the same way. The apostle Paul refers to unbelievers who are without God and without hope in the world. For such unhappy individuals, death represents the ultimate, unconquerable enemy.

But this is not Anne's concern. She does not fear the prospect of meeting her Maker. She knew that she was clothed in the righteousness of Christ. Her concern was of another kind. She would be as distressed, and in the same way, if she were having to sail for China. The concern was extended (not eternal) separation from her loved ones. "And the writer's pangs arise, not from dread of what lies after death, but from the thought of leaving a husband she loves and children half-reared."[52]

In other words, faced with the prospect of death, Anne was tender for the well-being of others. And in this tenderness, she exhibits her strength.

But for many moderns, tenderness is nonexistent unless it is applied indiscriminately. This view neglects, among other things, the way God made the world. It is assumed that if someone is tender at all, they must be universally tender. For example, take this misinformed comment. "In liberal ideas and toleration, she was far ahead of her cold, crusty, Puritan surrounding; with her former minister, John Cotton, she gave sympathy to Ann[sic] Hutchinson . . ."[53]

Anne Bradstreet's tenderness is obvious. But to be tender of everyone in a fallen world is actually to be cruel. To be tender of the lambs is to be tender. To be tender with the wolves is to be cruel to the lambs. This is why Christ was tender of the little children who were brought to him, and He was tender to lepers. He was not at all tender with the Pharisees.

Of course, in one sense, it is probably true that Anne was sympathetic to Anne Hutchinson. She was not the kind of person to bear personal malice toward anyone, regardless of how caught up in error that person might have been. The apostle Paul notes that there are enemies of the cross of Christ, but he says this with tears. His tears do not mean he is sympathetic to the heresy, but he is anguished over the situation.

We know that Anne was extremely tender toward and fully sympathetic of her father, her husband, *and* their work. Part of their work was restraining women like Anne Hutchinson. But one modern writer went so far as to fantasize about how Anne Bradstreet let her husband have it after he came home from a day of dealing with Anne Hutchinson. This sort of historical imagination is simply irresponsible.

So her tenderness was a biblical tenderness. She was a woman who was informed by biblical categories. Tolerating one another's faults and failings is a Christian virtue because love does cover a multitude of sins. But tolerating that woman Jezebel, as the apostle John put it, is no virtue at all.

As much as many contemporary writers might hate to admit it, Anne Bradstreet was a representative "cold and crusty" Puritan. This is not to say that every Puritan attained to her gifts and graces. It is probably fair to say that she surpassed a number of her contemporaries in achieving this difficult balance between strength and tenderness. But with this said, the entire Puritan community admired her achievement very much. She was not spurned for her "liberalism" and "compromise." She was admired by virtually everyone for her graces.

SHREWD

ANNE WAS a shrewd woman. She was not simple or naive, but she examined the issues of life carefully. But before developing this line of thought, perhaps it would be good to define exactly what is meant here by *shrewd*.

Shrewdness is wisdom in a homely setting. A shrewd observation is one that is likely to become proverbial. A wise professor might tell you not to take on more than you can handle. A shrewd uncle would tell you not to become a baker if your head's made of butter. A lofty bit of good advice might be to do your work right the first time. A shrewd grandmother might tell you about the fellow she once knew who was two hours getting his shirt on, and then he didn't get it right.

Shrewdness in this context does not mean sharp business dealings or craftiness in personal relationships.

By contrast, this is a holy shrewdness, a pleasant, amiable, and pointed awareness of how God made the world.

Anne Bradstreet had this gift of shrewd observation and insight. "Ambitious men are like hops that never rest climbing so long as they have anything to stay upon, but take away their props, and they are of all the most dejected."[54] One of the glories of this kind of statement is that it is very difficult to comment on. The thing is said so clearly and so well that any additional "clarification" is bringing coals to Newcastle.

Moreover, shrewdness is also wisdom in a *community* setting. Aristotle says somewhere that giftedness in metaphor is a mark of genius. If this is the case, we can see a communal genius in the collective proverbial wisdom of our people. Cursing the weather is bad farming.

Anne Bradstreet knew how the world went around. In her poem on the various ages of man, she described the sins and folly of youth in this way:

> *From pipe to pot, from pot to words and blows,*
> *For he that loveth wine wanteth no woes.*
> *Whole nights with ruffins, roarers, fiddlers spend,*
> *To all obscenity mine ears I lend.*[55]

The kids of this era were not into skateboarding and probably didn't have tattoos and baggy pants, but for the proverbially wise, nothing ever changes. She is speaking here of young people who are living a dissolute lifestyle and who cannot be corrected. They are wise in their own eyes and cannot see their own approaching ruin.

A shrewd wisdom, incidentally, can distinguish this from what might be called normal highjinks. In 1672, Anne's two youngest sons had a brush with the county court. John, when he was twenty, got in trouble for "smoking late at night" with some of his friends. Dudley and Nathaniel Wade (his future brother-in-law) had a scrape for "shooting pistols and drinking in the Quartermaster's house."[56] Both John and Dudley, however, went on to live fruitful, orderly, and sober lives.

Part of her practical wisdom—her shrewdness—can be seen in the fact that one of her favorite books in the Bible was Ecclesiastes. There the preacher comments repeatedly on the fact that all "under the sun" was vanity and grasping after wind. The book is one of profound, albeit realistic, optimism. The hope generated in this book is connected to the sovereignty of God, and not to *any* earthly circumstance. Anne Bradstreet also knew that "mortal helps are brittle dust."[57]

Anne knew as well the importance of discipline in the life of practical wisdom. As she put it, "I can no more live without correction than without food."[58] Those who would not accept correction had embraced the opposite of a godly shrewdness. "Harsh discipline is for him who forsakes the way, and he who hates correction will die" (Prov. 15:10). Parents should teach their children wisdom, both in what they say and in how they correct and spank. Children learn wisdom through the ears and the bottom.

But a fool rejects the wisdom inherent in correction. The ambitious man, climbing like hops, cannot be interrupted in order to listen to any warning. When his props are removed, he cannot be raised from his despondency to learn the explanation. The young fool who has just enough money to go drinking tonight is one who will not listen. He rejects correction which, to Anne Bradstreet, was the same as rejecting all food.

Someone who is shrewd cannot be readily stampeded into error or confusion, even when many others may demand it. There is an important *stability* in this kind of wisdom. Although the hysteria of the Salem witch trials occurred after Anne's death, her husband, who shared this same kind of wisdom with her, was a courageous opponent of those trials.[59]

Doctrinal

O NE OF the themes in this book is to save Anne Bradstreet from those who would save her from her own theology. "In the end, these doubts and misgivings were always conquered, not so much by a conscientious loyalty to Puritan dogma as by an essential faith in 'this Rock Christ Jesus' and the certainty that 'he is able to keep that [which] I have committed to his charge.'"[60]

Of course, this observation overlooks the fact that a central tenet of Puritan dogma was the necessity of looking in faith to the Rock Christ Jesus.

Those who write about Anne Bradstreet admit that she held to Puritan convictions, because ultimately they have to. The evidence for this is overwhelming. But because she was such an admirable woman, they generally want her to have not meant it somehow. This is particularly the case when it comes to a doctrine near the center of Puritan theology—the doctrine of God's sovereign election. Anne Bradstreet was *surrounded* by people who thought and taught this, and so some of her expressions naturally have picked up hints of this, etc.

But consider how she spoke of it:

> *All the works and doings of God are wonderful, but none more awful than His great work of election and reprobation; when we consider how many good parents have had bad children, and again how many bad parents have had pious children, it should make us adore the sovereignty of God, who will not be tied to time nor place, nor yet to persons, but takes and chooses, when and where and whom He pleases; it should also teach the children of godly parents to walk with fear and trembling, lest they through unbelief fall short of a promise; it may also be a support to such as have or had wicked parents, that if they abide not in unbelief, God is able to gaff them in. The upshot of all should make us with the apostle to admire the justice and mercy of God and say how unsearchable are His ways and His footsteps past finding out.*[61]

Anne did not try to solve the mystery of God's sovereignty and man's free agency. Her response was one of worship and admiration. "There is nothing admits of more admiration than God's various dispensation of His gifts among the sons of men . . . and no other reason can be given of all this but so it pleased Him whose will is the perfect rule of righteousness."[62]

This approach is the one enjoined by John Calvin himself. "O the height and the depth! You ask a reason. I stand in awe before the height and depth. You rationate, I admire; you dispute, I believe. I see the height, but I do not comprehend the depth. Paul rests quietly because he found wonder. He calls the judgments of God inscrutable—do you mean to scrutinize them? He says His ways are past finding out—do you propose to find them out?"[63]

Anne Bradstreet completely accepted the teaching of man's depravity—as a result of Adam's rebellion—as well as God's gracious sovereignty. Moreover, she incorporated them into her thinking and poetry.

> *How Adam sighed to see his progeny,*
> *Clothed all in his black sinful livery.*[64]

As a result of Adam's rebellion, we are all born in sin.

> *Stained from birth with Adam's sinful fact,*
> *Thence I began to sin as soon to act.*[65]

From this understanding of man's radical depravity, all the Puritan doctrines about God's sovereignty in salvation necessarily follow. Anne Bradstreet knew this and did not shrink back from the doctrinal ramifications of it.

This was not because she was shrill or doctrinaire. It was because she was a biblical woman who lived among a biblical people. "The Bible was the air she and everyone else breathed."[66]

She did not see this as sectarian, or divisive. It was simply orthodoxy—what the Bible taught. But for her, this was not a grim, distasteful truth. The God who ordains everything, and who directs everything to its appointed end, is a God of unspeakable glory and majesty. She did not assume, as many do, that to give glory to God somehow takes glory away from God. In one of her poems, in speaking of the brightness of the sun, she comments, "How full of glory then must thy Creator be."[67]

This is how she lived and died—concerned to affirm with her lips what the Word and all nature declares. She wanted her "doctrine" to be the same as that taught by the sun.

Humor and Irony

*T*HE HUMOR of Anne Bradstreet is certainly not boisterous or of a slapstick variety. But in her expressions and turns of phrase, the reader can see she has a clear ability with what might be called amiable irony.

In her meditations, she comments on spurious conviction of sin. "We often see stones hang with drops not from any innate moisture, but from a thick air about them; so may we sometimes see marble-hearted sinners seem full of contrition, but it is not from any dew of grace within but from some black cloud that impends them, which produces these sweating effects."[68]

Of course, the point she is making is quite a serious one. But the reader has a hard time thinking of these "sweating effects" on marble hearts without smiling at the comment.

She also had something to say about how some Christians are reluctant to allow God to wean them off certain blessings. "Some children are hardly weaned; although the teat be rubbed with wormwood or mustard, they will either wipe it off, or else suck down sweet and bitter together. So is it with some Christians: let God embitter all the sweets of this life, that so they might feed upon more substantial food, yet they are so childishly sottish that they are still hugging and sucking these empty breasts that God is forced to hedge up their way with thorns or lay affliction on their loins so that they might shake hands with the world, before it bid them farewell."[69]

Anne was able to maintain the objectivity of ironic detachment without falling into cynicism. And while she does not have the biting wit of Nathaniel Ward, her wit nonetheless has a presence that can make itself known.

Elizabeth Wade White captures this aspect of Anne's personality well. She refers to "the tenderness and concern that animate the whole poem [eight birds poem] make one feel that Anne Bradstreet must have been a delightful parent (as well as a conscientious disciplinarian), sympathetic and understanding, humorous and sometimes even gay, a sharer of learning and a teacher of wisdom, whose unfailing love for her children was reflected in the love and respect that they felt for her and in the good and fruitful lives that all of them seem to have led."[70]

Much is being said here, but the words *delightful*, *humorous*, and *gay* stand out. The Bible teaches us that we are to adorn our doctrine with the kind of lives we lead. And this is what Anne Bradstreet did. Her graciousness and the winsomeness of her wit were endearing to all those who knew her, and her children knew her particularly well. Laughter and gladness are not really detachable from genuine Christian living.

At the same time, we live in a fallen world, and our gladness must live next door to folly and evil, and sometimes this can result in a fairly grim humor. Earlier in this book, we addressed the history of the downfall of Archbishop Laud and his friend Strafford, persecutors of the saints. Strafford was beheaded some time before Laud was, and Anne Bradstreet was not too refined to take a hard look at it.

> *Which by their prudence stood them in such stead*
> *They took high Strafford lower by the head.*[71]

This is not hypocrisy or inconsistency. The humor of the saints is sometimes severe and sometimes kind and tender. The Lord Jesus had no problem making jokes at the expense of that day's respected theologians—those owners and managers of the Blind Guide Site Seeing Service. Nor did Paul have difficulty chiding those bellygods who refused to worship a deity more than six inches above their large intestine.

But when the Lord speaks to the woman at the well, He teases her (much more mildly than this) about her marital history. "You are quite right to say you have no husband. *That*, at least, was accurate. You have had five, and are currently using a spare."

Anne Bradstreet was committed to wisdom and consequently could see the humor in folly. But she was also personally humble, and she did not have a problem with making pointed observations at her own expense. In this she was following the biblical pattern. A scriptural Christian knows how to take the truth seriously without taking himself too seriously. When the cause of the Lord gets all tangled up in whatever it is that we want to do, a serious confusion has occurred.

Anne was objective enough to see herself as she was, but not so "objective" that she tried to examine the Word of God from some supposedly neutral position. Her balance at this point is clearly seen in the kind of thing she found humorous.

INTELLIGENT

LTHOUGH ANNE BRADSTREET was a committed Puritan, her faith in these doctrines was not unthinking, reflexive, or doctrinaire. She thought through what she believed, and she did not commit herself to anything unless she really did believe it.

We have already noted how her "heart rose" over the issue of whether to join the church at Boston. At issue in that situation was not the fundamental doctrines of the faith but rather what we might call some of the *distinctives* of the church at Boston. Anne was not prepared to assent to them unless she was convinced that what they were requiring was, in fact, the truth of God. After she was convinced, she assented, but not until then.

As the colony grew in numbers, other controversies arose, and these presented new questions. We have already considered Anne's response to Roger Williams and Anne Hutchinson—she was clearly on the side of her father and her husband in those confrontations. But at the same time, turmoil that unsettled the whole colony was certain to have raised questions in the mind of any thinking individual. And Anne was such a person. But one of the most important things to consider is what kind of issues were raised. In a probable reference to these troubles, as she looked back over her life, she put it this way:

"But some new troubles I have had since the world has been filled with blasphemy and sectaries, and some who have been accounted sincere Christians have been carried away with them, that sometimes I have said, 'Is there faith upon the earth?' . . . I know whom I have trusted, and whom I have believed, and that He is able to keep that [which] I have committed to His charge."[72]

Several things are important here. Anne clearly identifies the problems for what they are—blasphemy and sectarianism. The problem is caused by those who are vulnerable to various heresies. She notes that some who were accounted sincere Christians were carried off by the sectaries. Her problem was comparable to Paul at Antioch when "even Barnabas," as he put it, was carried off by the error. The thing she wonders is not whether the sectaries are right, but whether or not there is any true faithfulness on the earth. She resolves the question by committing herself to God.

As she works through these issues, she is clearly *thinking*. Her commitment to the truth was tested by the disruptions, and she did not resolve the disruptions by refusing to think but rather through trusting in God.

In a similar way, she describes some of her occasions of greater doubt. The fact that there was a God was immediately obvious to her—all she had to do was look around. But what about other religions? What about Roman Catholicism? For thinking individuals, one of the first questions that arises is the epistemological question. How do we know what we know? In a religious context, how do we know that our faith is the right one? Doesn't everyone think that? Why am I special?

Among other things, Anne resolves this question by doing what Jesus commanded—she considered the fruit. The Roman church of her day can only be described as bloodthirsty, for it had the blood of thousands of Protestant saints to account for. In the end she knows herself to be a creature, and so she commits herself to God. And, she says, if I perish, I perish.

There is nothing particularly intelligent about doubting. But intelligence can be revealed in how the doubts are raised and then answered. She does not refuse to raise the question the way an unthinking dogmatist might refuse to do. At the same time, she does refuse to question outside the boundaries of rational inquiry, the way an unthinking skeptic loves to do. Because she knows herself to be a creature, with limitations, she raises the question. Because she knows herself to be a creature, with limitations, she does not attempt to answer questions which only omniscience can answer.

In her poem on flesh and spirit, she knows how to pose the question. Flesh taunts the spirit as, no doubt, her flesh had done before.

> *Dost dream of things beyond the moon,*
> *And dost thou hope to dwell there soon?*[73]

Spirit answers faithfully, and Anne shows that she is familiar with the argument. At the same time (creaturely), flesh is not to be denied as though matter were somehow sinful. The Christian view of the subduing of the flesh is not to be confused with stoicism.

> *Such stoics are but stocks, such teaching vain,*
> *While man is man, he shall have ease or pain.*[74]

Anne held to the truth, not as an impersonal block of wood, but as a faithful Christian woman.

EDUCATED

$\mathcal{A}$ s WE have noted a number of times, Anne Bradstreet was highly educated. But her education was an issue for various reasons, and in some respects, it was an issue for the whole colony. As we shall see, the fact that she had such a good testimony as a woman of great learning was tremendously important.

Obviously, "the unnerving performance of Anne Hutchinson had disordered the colony in 1636."[75] And Winthrop, about ten years later, wrote of a woman in New England whose learning had driven her mad. He said the madness was "by occasion of her giving herself wholly to reading and writing, and [she had] written many books."[76] This husband had been indulgent of his wife's bookishness, according to Winthrop's account, and by the time he saw his error, it was too late to do anything about it.

In addition, there had been a problem within the Dudley household. Anne's younger sister, Sarah, married a Major Benjamin Keanye. They returned to England from America for business, and the first sign of trouble was a letter from "Stephen Winthrop (whose sister Mary had married Samuel Dudley) to his brother John Winthrop, Jr."[77] In the letter, he mentions cryptically that "Cosin Keane is growne a great preacher."

Benjamin Keanye soon wrote Thomas Dudley a series of letters, accusing Anne's sister of gross immorality and charging her as well with various religious irregularities. In the last of the letters, Major Keanye resolved never to live with her as a husband again. The general court in Massachusetts granted a divorce, and, shortly afterward, the church at Boston excommunicated Sarah for "Irregular Prophecying," and for having fallen into lewd and scandalous behaviour with an excommunicated person.[78]

Thomas Dudley apparently convinced the authorities that his daughter was mentally irresponsible rather than openly rebellious, and herein lies the problem. Presumably, Sarah had been taught and educated the same way that Anne had been, and what was to keep tongues from wagging as a result? What was to prevent those who would say that women ought not to be tempted through education?

In large part, the centerpiece of the answer to those who took this view was named Anne Bradstreet. "Anne Bradstreet's life was a model of graciousness and devotion; her deep love for her kindred was as deeply returned, and she was apparently respected by all who really knew her."[79]

But the stakes were still high. If there were those who maintained that education was a destroyer of women, and if they were to make their case, they would have to explain Anne. There she was, a devoted wife and mother, a dutiful daughter, and a learned writer of poetry. Not only was she a published writer, but her poems covered the waterfront. She wrote about politics, history, medicine, theology, and so on. And she did so with a level of expertise for each subject. She lived in a house that was filled with books. "The Bradstreet library of over eight hundred books (destroyed along with some of the poet's manuscripts on July 12, 1666, when the house burned) showed the family's affluence and scholarliness."[80]

Not only that, but she had also grown up in and around nobility, and she had access to many books. She most certainly had a well-furnished mind. And this well-furnished mind was also a very balanced and stable mind. Those who would explain the instability of some of the women in the colony would have to find a culprit other than education. Anne was a living refutation.

If it were maintained that *some* women ought not to be educated because of their instability, the answer would be that this applies equally to men. Are there no unstable men? Are there no men who handle the stuff of learning badly? No, the argument against women and education only works if it can be shown to be a universally bad idea. And Anne Bradstreet made that position impossible.

Not only so, but her learning appears to have *equipped* her in various ways to be a more effective wife and mother. Her education was more than innocuous—it was positively helpful. She was given to the domestic priorities, and she saw her learning as ally in this. Today's equivalent would be high school girls' using trig to help them with quilting patterns and other sewing projects.

If education, considered as such, was not the problem with some of these women, then what was? First, to answer within the biblical framework, the central problem is sin. Anne would have resisted any attempt to locate the problem in the external circumstances. To the extent that circumstances presented temptations, we may point to unsettled pioneer life and the political and social turmoil back in England. And to the extent women gave way to such temptations, we would have to say the problem was a sinful heart—coupled with a *lack* of education.

FAMILY

*A*NNE BRADSTREET belonged to an *interesting* family. Her father was a courageous man of integrity who sometimes collided with other courageous men of integrity. There was, for example, "political tension between [Anne's] father and Governor Winthrop."[81]

Dudley was accused by Winthrop of "usury in the sale of corn" and of overdecorating his house. Angered by this, Dudley resigned his deputy governorship, but the general court refused to accept it. The two men were both good guys, and they knew reconciliation was important, and it was apparently achieved. The "marriage of Winthrop's daughter Mary to Samuel Dudley, the deputy's oldest child, in this same year of 1632, seems to have brought about a genuine reconciliation."[82]

The spirits in the Dudley clan ran high, however. After Anne's mother died, her father married again, and a much younger half-brother, Joseph, was born. Cotton Mather, in his great history of New England, was not able to write as fully about Thomas Dudley as he would have liked, and this was because of Joseph. "Mather was not on friendly terms with the then head of the family, the ambitious politician Joseph Dudley, Thomas's eldest son by his second marriage."[83] Mather had to apologize for the brevity of his account of Thomas Dudley's life. The Dudleys didn't want anything published about their clan without their approval, and Mather was apparently not in a position to get it.

Joseph Dudley had an interesting career. He "made influential friends at court and in Parliamentary circles, and in 1685 was commissioned by King James II as president of the colonies of Maine, New Hampshire, Massachusetts, and Rhode Island."[84] This was not really appreciated in New England, however. During the reign of James II, the affairs of New England were grossly managed by the Andros government, and Joseph Dudley was part of it. But when "news came of the abdication of James II and the accession of King William and Queen Mary, in the spring of 1689, the Andros government was briskly overturned and the leaders, including Joseph Dudley, were imprisoned for some months in Boston and then deported to England."[85]

Joseph was a man of parts and abilities, and he fared well back in England. He became the lieutenant governor of the Isle of Wight, was elected to Parliament, and eventually returned to Massachusetts in 1702 as governor. He had apparently learned something and governed without incident.

But when Anne's lordly half-brother was run off the first time, the man the colony turned to in order to restore order was Simon Bradstreet, now eighty-seven. He was by that time "the Nestor of New England," as Mather called him. He served until 1692.

One of the great difficulties in Massachusetts was the turmoil created by what was called the Half-way Covenant. In a mistaken zeal for the purity of the church, the Puritans required too much for membership in the church. Although they practiced infant baptism, they still required some kind of marked conversion "experience" before someone could be admitted to the Lord's Supper. As a result, many baptized children grew up on the colony without ever becoming communicant members of the church. The problem was created when *they* got married, started having children, and wanted to have *their* children baptized. This was allowed, and it was called the Half-way covenant. Far from being a degradation of standards of covenant purity, it was the direct result of having artificially high standards. The Bible requires a confession that Jesus is Lord, and the absence of a scandalous lifestyle. It does not require a convulsive Damascus road experience on the part of every convert, especially those who have been nurtured in a covenant home.

This came to a head after the rule of Cromwell. After the restoration of the monarchy, Simon was one of the delegates who went to Charles II to have the colony's charter renewed. This was done, but one of the conditions was that no one could be banned from the Supper except for scandalous practices. Simon agreed with this, and generally supported "the broadening of ecclesiastical standards."[86]

This agreement was badly received in New England, but Simon Bradstreet took everything in stride. Simon married again, four years after Anne's death, in June of 1676. He married another Anne, the widow of Captain Joseph Gardner of Salem, who was killed in the Indian war called King Philip's War in 1675.

After this marriage, Simon went to live in Salem, where he distinguished himself in his opposition to the brief aberration of the witch trials. In this, Simon Bradstreet stood with *most* of the leaders and ministers of New England. But the local hysteria in Salem could not be stopped because there was no governor at the time. When a duly appointed governor arrived, he was pressured by the Puritan ministers of New England to stop the trials, which he did.

Simon Bradstreet became deputy governor in 1678. The next year he was elected governor, and he served from 1679 to 1686. After the fall of James II, he became governor again and ruled from 1689 to 1692. He died peacefully, old and full of years, at the age of ninety-four.

LONG-SUFFERING

REMINDERS ARE good. Longsuffering is still a better word than our modern substitute for it—patience. While *patience* can cover certain dire situations, it can also refer to waiting "patiently" for someone who is five minutes late for an appointment.

As a number of her poems testify, Anne Bradstreet had recurring bouts of illness that drastically affected her ability to work at her duties as a wife and mother. Through her suffering, two themes in her writing stand out. The first is the need for a Christian to be satisfied in the will of God, regardless of what that will happens to be. Samuel Rutherford once expressed the biblical attitude toward suffering when he said that when he was in the cellar of affliction, he looked for God's choicest wines. The second theme is the need to express thanksgiving and gratitude for all the blessings God provides, particularly the blessing of deliverance from suffering when it is given.

In the midst of her own sufferings, Anne spoke about it this way: "After much weaknes and sicknes when my spirits were worn out, and many times my faith weak likewise, the Lord was pleased to uphold my drooping heart, and to manifest his Love to me . . ."[87]

And immediately afterward, when she was restored to health, she wrote a poem of joy and thanksgiving where she expresses "gratitude to her maker" and "her pleasure in the beauty of the season." She did not take her restoration for granted at all.[88]

And so Anne Bradstreet was long-suffering in her temptations and trials, and she was extremely grateful when God brought her out of the trials. And further, she thoroughly understood *why* God dealt with His servants in this fashion. "Corn, till it have past through the mill and been ground to powder, is not fit for bread. God so deals with his servants: he grinds them with grief and pain till they turn to dust, and then are they fit manchet for his mansions."[89] Manchet is a small roll or loaf of the very finest wheat bread. The flour has to be ground fine if the bread is to be fine. As the old blues song put it, everybody wants to go to heaven, but nobody wants to die. It would be lovely, we think, to be the finest bread that heaven holds, but we do not want to be ground to powder. We want to be exalted without being humbled, but the Christian faith does not teach this. Even our Lord was not given the name above every name until after He had humbled Himself to the point of death on the cross.

The metaphor of grinding wheat may change although the central experience does not. "Iron, till it be thoroughly heat, is uncapable to be wrought; so God sees good to cast some men into the furnace of affliction and then beats them on His anvil into what frame he pleases."[90] In the Bible, suffering has a point—it is the prelude to glory.

Anne exhibited this trait in more than just medical afflictions. When their house burned to the ground, Anne had to surrender to the goodness of God in this hard providence:

> *And when I could no longer look,*
> *I blest His name who gave and took,*
> *That laid my goods now in the dust.*
> *Yea, so it was, and so 'twas just.*[91]

We also see that her gratitude put her suffering into perspective. When we chafe and rebel in our sufferings, we only prolong them and make them worse. There is no situation so bad that we, through a bad attitude, cannot make it worse. But when we give thanks for all things as the Bible instructs, and we acknowledge that all things *do* work together for good for the saints of God, we discover that the burdens have been greatly lightened. And this is what we see in Anne's experience. Although she had suffered a great deal—through illness, trouble with her sister, the deaths of grandchildren, the loss of a house—she did not do what the flesh always want to do—complain that *this* situation is unique, and that nobody understands what I have to suffer. She said, "I have found by experience that I can no more live without correction than without food . . . I have not been refined in the furnace of affliction as some have been, but have rather been preserved with sugar than brine."[92] She knew that God was being kind to her in her great afflictions; consequently, she had the perspective that her great afflictions *were* great kindnesses. She thought of her sufferings as sugar, not brine.

A complaining spirit can make unhappiness out of anything, and a long-suffering patience can find joy anywhere.

PATRIOTIC

*A*NNE BRADSTREET was a patriotic English-woman. She loved her home country and was distraught at the turmoil that threatened it. In this love, she was not a mindless partisan.

In political controversies, the ever present temptation is to divide into two camps, with all the good guys on our side (and nothing but good guys), and all the bad guys over on the other side. A clear sign of a thinking patriot in the midst of civil controversy is when wickedness on your side is acknowledged and decency on the other side is similarly acknowledged. In other words, even when an issue comes down to a war, and one must choose which side he is on, he is still able to make subtle distinctions. Anne Bradstreet, along with others in her circle, exhibited exactly this kind of civic wisdom.

This type of moderation, however, must not be confused with the moderation we are accustomed to in our day, a moderation that refuses to make any fundamental distinctions at all. For example, as a Puritan who loved her nation, she identified the central problem as the temptations presented by Rome. She recognized that the turmoil in England was *constitutionally* complex, but it was nevertheless *religiously* simple.

> *And for myself let miseries abound,*
> *If mindless of thy state I e'er be found.*
> *These are the days the Church's foes to crush,*
> *To root out Popelings head, tail, branch, and rush;*
> *Let's bring Baal's vestments forth to make a fire,*
> *Their miters, surplices, and all their tire,*
> *Copes, rochets, crosiers, and such empty trash,*
> *And let their names consume, but let the flash*
> *Light Christendom, and all the world to see*
> *We hate Rome's whore with all her trumpery.*[93]

At issue was whether or not England would worship God according to His Word. In noting this, we must remember that religious issues in that day were not part of our modern denominational system. Spain and France were Catholic powers, and they were a very real threat to Protestant England. Compromise with Roman Catholicism at any level was consequently a political issue and quite possibly a matter of treason. Civil and ecclesiastical issues were all tangled together. Probably the only modern situation that compares to this is the current impasse in Northern Ireland. Economic, political, historical, and

religious matters are all mixed up together. Anne Bradstreet saw that if England was to be free, England had to
be Protestant. Moreover, to be halfheartedly Protestant
was to be halfheartedly free.

Anne Bradstreet was not just willing to *say* that she
loved her nation and people. In order to maintain civic
blessing, she was also willing for the sacrifices that had
to be made by her and by her household. Simon Bradstreet's many absences from the home were the result of
public business, laboring for the good of the colony. This
was extremely hard on Anne, but she acknowledged it
as part of her duty as well.

The clearest example of this occurred when Charles II
was brought back to the throne after Cromwell's Interreg-
num. Simon Bradstreet was chosen, along with John
Norton, to act as emissary to the king, seeking a renewal
of the colony's charter. The details of that trip will be discussed in greater detail later, but for Anne, it meant a long
separation from Simon, coupled with the dangers of him
having to cross the ocean twice. She was willing for this
because it was his duty, and therefore hers.

> *I in obedience to Thy will*
> *Thou knowest did submit.*
> *It was my duty so to do;*
> *O Lord accept of it.*[94]

The Puritans of New England had a good understanding of how the governments of family, church, and state
had to work together. To them a society was more than a
collection of individuals. Duties and responsibilities were

mutual. Households made up the church and state, and both of those entities acknowledged the importance of the household.

They were all covenanted together. While the social fabric that exhibited this covenant in Puritan New England did not last, the example provided by it *did* last. Anne's love for her homeland was not a separated love, detached from her commitment to the truth as preached faithfully by the church or her commitment to her husband.

She loved her nation the way every nation should be loved—in context.

CULTURAL

*T*HE PURITANS were an educated, culturally refined people. Their ministers led the way in a rejection of an ornate cultural expression in preaching. For example, in his early years John Cotton was a great preacher in the university style, decorating his sermons with literary quotations and so forth. But he came to the conclusion that this was not how the Word was to be preached, and he turned to a simple exposition of the text—to the great displeasure of some of his refined listeners, who wanted some literary fireworks.

When the Puritans rejected this erudite expression in favor of the "plain style," they were not doing this as fundamentalist anti-intellectuals. They were fully capable of competing with their Anglican adversaries in this fashion. Murdock comments on the Puritan recognition of English religious literature in his time. "Some of it he read and approved, much of it he suspected or disliked, but he knew a great deal about most of it."[95] Theirs was not an ignorant opposition. But they believed the Word of God did not derive its power from human ornamentation, and that, in many cases, to add such ornamentation was to dilute the Word.

But it would be a great mistake to assume that the Puritans were indifferent to literary or cultural issues. The New England Puritans were genuinely concerned with aesthetic values in their writing. The Puritan "kept at his task, studied diligently both books and men, and ultimately created a body of literature which was, considering the circumstances, extraordinary in bulk and contained many pages of genuine artistic excellence."[96]

The Puritans were wary about cultural delights, not because they opposed them necessarily, but because in every delightful created thing, a temptation to idolatry existed. And idolatry, they knew, was deeply unsatisfying. Anne Bradstreet put it this way. "The treasures of this world may well be compared to husks, for they have no kernal in them, and they that feed upon them may soon stuff their throats, but cannot fill their bellies. They may be choked by them, but cannot be satisfied with them."[97]

But at the same time, the Puritans believed that cultural achievement was a lawful activity, and, if lawful, it had to be done to the glory of God. "But a Puritan's duty to achieve success was a part of his duty to God."[98] The success was required in whatever field God had called him to. So to the extent that the Puritans were involved in the world of letters, they believed they were required to recognize excellence where it occurred and to achieve it themselves where possible.

This attitude can be seen in Anne's eulogy of Sir Philip Sidney. He was the quintessential Elizabethan courtier, highly respected throughout England. He was not a thoroughgoing Puritan, but respect for him was possible in a Puritan context. But it was still complicated. Sidney's love for "Stella" was adulterous, and, of course, the biblical Puritans would not applaud this in any way. But for cultural Puritans, distinctions were necessary. Anne's poem on Sidney, in part, reads this way:

> *Which makes severer eyes but slight that story,*
> *And men of morose minds envy his glory.*
> *But he's a beetle-head that can't descry*
> *A world of wealth within that rubbish lie.*[99]

Yes, Sidney's work contained rubbish. But those who would reject the loveliness contained in his work because of that rubbish are categorized nicely by Anne Bradstreet—"beetleheads." It is the part of wisdom to refuse to go pearl diving in a cesspool, but only folly, only a beetlewit, would walk by a pile of pearls because a few of them were dirty.

So Anne Bradstreet defends the reading and appreciation of Sidney despite some of the questionable material. And while she does not overtly defend the reading of Chaucer and Shakespeare, there are indications in her work that she was familiar with both.

This is in line with the typical Puritan attitude. "The Puritans knew the difference between 'studied plainness, and negligent rudeness.'"[100] The Puritans valued clarity over beauty, but within the context of their aesthetic theory, this is simply a way of saying they preferred the beauty of clarity to the beauty of ornament.

This was the context of Anne's cultural accomplishment. Anne Bradstreet was a significant poet, but in the literary world, she was still a minor poet. In this accomplishment, she was not overcoming the Puritan hostility to literary excellence. We have to remember that she was a minor literary figure even within the ranks of Puritanism—which, we should remember, contained men like John Milton, Edmund Spenser, and Andrew Marvell.

Disciplinarian

ANNE BRADSTREET understood the importance of discipline throughout the Christian life, and particularly she saw the need for it in the home. In a fallen world, good things do not happen automatically by themselves. A man who desires a garden full of weeds does not need to do anything.

Anne did not believe that the reason for disciplining children was because that was what children needed. She believed in it because that was the way the world was. One of her comments on this is worth reproducing at length:

> Corn is produced with much labour (as the hus-
> bandman well knows), and some land asks much
> more pains than some other doth to be brought into

> *tilth; yet all must be ploughed and harrowed. Some*
> *children (like sour land) are of so tough and morose*
> *a disposition that the plough of correction must*
> *make long furrows on their back and the harrow of*
> *discipline go often over them before they be fit soil*
> *to sow the seed of morality much less of grace in*
> *them. But when by prudent nurture they are*
> *brought into a fit capacity, let the seed of good*
> *instruction and exhortation be sown in the spring of*
> *their youth, and a plentiful crop may be expected in*
> *the harvest of their years."* [101]

Her approach to discipline was matter-of-factual. She knew that discipline was essential. But here, as in so many other areas, she did not take a simplistic "one-size-fits-all" approach. Some children need to be disciplined sternly before they can be fitted for anything. Others do not require the same treatment.

Anne Bradstreet did not believe what many Christian parents today seem to believe—i.e., that each child starts his or her life at the same place. Children are not a *tabula rasa*, a blank slate, on which the experiences of life are written. Some children, like certain patches of ground, are rockier than others. Such children require parents who are willing to take more pains over them. If a farmer has two patches of ground, one of rich topsoil and the other filled with rocks, he cannot treat the two patches of ground the same way.

Discipline is corrective, unlike punishment. When a magistrate executes a criminal, this is a matter of retributive justice. He is not attempting to discipline the criminal;

that is, he is not trying to make him any better. The execution is a matter of justice, simple punishment.

But parents who discipline their children are trying to correct them. They discipline them on the same principles they apply when they put their children into the bathtub. If one child is filthy, he might have to spend more time in the tub. His brother, who did not get quite so grimy, will not be required to spend the same amount of time there "in the interest of fairness." Consequently, under the oversight of a wise parent, the discipline applied to children will vary according to their condition.

And it should also be noted that Anne referred to a distinction between civic morality and grace. A mother who disciplines her children is preparing them for one or two things, and hopefully both. A child who is disciplined well is being fitted for a useful and moral life in human society. But a child can be disciplined in this way without any experience of saving grace. The morality exhibited is from God—what theologians call common grace—but it does not put that individual right with God. That does not happen until an individual is born again.

Anne knew that godly parents were engaged in preparation for both social morality and saving grace. When grace came to a covenant child, it was not a lightning bolt from on high. God in His sovereignty uses means, and one of the common means He uses to bring children into a saving relationship with Himself is the wisdom and love shown in gracious and wise discipline. This is why Anne saw it necessary to discipline children as a means of plowing the soil before attempting to plant anything. If these children are not plowed up with discipline, they are not "fit soil to sow the seed of morality much less of grace in them."

Morality is a seed that grows, but only in prepared soil. Grace is also a different kind of seed that grows, but like civic morality it grows in prepared soil. As both grow up, they are measured in the result. "Yellow leaves argue want of sap and gray hairs want of moisture; so dry and sapless performances are symptoms of little spiritual vigor."[102]

But often the result is poor because the preparation was poor. The growth is poor because the soil was never tilled. The soil was never tilled because parents were not diligent to do what must always be done in the home.

Discipline is not the same thing as growth. Anne was wiser than to think so. Only God gives the increase. But His Word declares that He commonly gives the increase under certain conditions. Paul plants and Apollo waters.

Virtuous

$\mathcal{P}$ERSONAL VIRTUE and integrity were important to Anne Bradstreet. She put the issue this way, with characteristic plainness: "That town which thousands of enemies without hath not been able to take hath been delivered up by one traitor within, and that man which all the temptations of Satan without could not hurt hath been foiled by one lust within."[103]

Internal lusts are traitors, and must be guarded against diligently. Moreover, they present much more of a threat than any open adversaries outside. Thousands of the enemy outside may assail the walls in vain, while one treacherous citizen inside can secretly open a door, and all is undone.

The Puritan did not believe that the world and the devil by themselves were the problem. He fought against the world, the *flesh*, and the devil. This is why the charge of self-righteousness, which is so commonly made against the Puritans, is such a false accusation. The Puritans were not taught to doubt the Word of God, but they were taught to doubt themselves. The man who accuses another without ever considering whether he is in some sense guilty is an arrogant man. It would be better to meet a bear robbed of her cubs than to meet such a fool in his folly. Jesus said to apply any judgments to ourselves that we make to others. To refuse to do so is hypocrisy.

This is something the Puritans did well. They were as wary about personal inconsistencies (treacheries from within) as they were about the rebellions of Archbishop Laud or Charles I. Those things that they opposed in the world were things that they opposed in themselves.

Having said all this, it is important to distinguish two senses of the word *world*. In Puritan thinking, the world could represent the world's way of thinking. This is what the apostle John was warning against when he said not to love the world, or the things in the world—the lusts of the flesh, the lusts of the eyes, and the pride of life (1 John 2:15–16). This is the world *system*.

But the problem is not the external, material world. The Puritans affirmed that the created order was good. But because man was sinful and fallen, when he saw the goodness of the material world and the order of it, his lusts caused him to "disorder" what he saw. The external world is not the problem, but because of sin, the external world does *present* a problem. Anne Bradstreet spoke of it this way:

The eyes and the ears are the inlets or doors of the soul, through which innumerable objects enter; yet is not that spacious room filled, neither doth it ever say it is enough, but like the daughters of the horse-leach, cries, 'Give, give'; and which is most strange, the more it receives, the more empty it finds itself and sees an impossibility ever to be filled but by Him in whom all fullness dwells.[104]

The more a man sees, the more he wants. The more he throws things into his soul, the emptier he gets. This is, as Anne says, "most strange." The nature of lust is to demand more and more of that which does not satisfy at all. It can only be described as a kind of frenzy.

When a man learns to deny himself, public virtue and usefulness become possible. When he gives way to himself and starts to throw consumer item after consumer item into the bottomless pit of his soul, he soon becomes quite occupied with the project, spending all his time on it. As Anne noted, this self-destructive process can begin with one lust treacherously opening the gates one time.

Those who truly understand temptation are those who stand up against it. If temptation were to be compared to the force of gale winds, the man who stands up against them knows far more about wind than the man who blows right over. The perfect example of this was the Lord Jesus—He understands temptation and sin far better than we do precisely because He never sinned. Sinning does not equip us to understand sinning.

Following the Lord, in a lesser way, those who are virtuous in this world understand the temptations to be unvirtuous far better than those who have succumbed to their temptations. The fellow lying on the ground thinks he knows all about the wind, but he does not.

By every account we have, Anne Bradstreet lived a life of exemplary virtue. She did not accomplish this because she somehow lived above the realm of temptation. She knew what it was to feel the force of the wind. But she also knew the importance of keeping her integrity. She knew the importance of keeping a watch out for all those internal traitors. She guarded her gates well, both without and within.

HOLY

THE GLORY of a Christian is to worship the Lord in the beauty of holiness. Of course, this is not possible apart from the grace of God. This holiness is best understood, not as a separate virtue, but rather as the meeting point of all the virtues and graces of an individual. Boldness and humility, love and justice, tenderness and joy, all meet together in a holy individual in a holy balance.

Anne Bradstreet knew that such holiness did not arise from within, but rather it was based upon communion with God. A person who is out of fellowship with God could not be holy, and someone in fellowship with God cannot be anything else. Everything hinges on the response to God. She put it this way. "It is a pleasant thing to behold the light, but sore eyes are not able to look upon it; the pure in heart shall see God, but the defiled in conscience shall rather choose to be buried under rocks and mountains than to behold the presence of the Lamb."[105]

Personal holiness was therefore a matter of walking with God—and not trying to accomplish things for God. Walking with God requires an eye of faith, where the individual can anticipate what it will be like to have eternal communion with Him. If they have this hope in them, people purify themselves. If they do not, then of course it will be easy to be unduly attached to the world of sense only. "The reason why Christians are so loath to exchange this world for a better is because they have more sense than faith: they see what they enjoy; they do but hope for that which is to come."[106] Faith looks at that which is not seen, but that which is eternal. Sense can only anticipate the next meal.

When someone is within the visible Church, and yet he does not walk in communion with God and so does not have this personal holiness, he is in an awkward position. He still has all the standards of the Christian faith (the law), but he does not experience the grace that enables him to live according to it. For the gracious heart, the law is no more constraining than wings are to a bird. But for someone who has no experience of grace, these standards bite and pinch, and some accommodation must be made for both morality and sin. Anne noted this problem clearly. "Some Christians do by their lusts and corruptions as the Israelites did by the Canaanites, not destroy them but put them under tribute."[107]

This leaves the professing Christian with the worst of both worlds. He has all the requirements of the faith and none of the joy, and has all the guilt of rebellion without complete abandonment to sin. "Sin and shame ever go together. He that would be freed from the last must be sure to shun the company of the first."[108]

But there are great cart and horse issues here. Communion with God through Christ drives out sin. Driving out sin for the sake of communion with God doesn't work. Salvation is all of grace. Of course, when we first come to Christ we must repent. But this repentance is not to be understood as "cleaning ourselves up for God." Rather, it should be thought of as understanding and submitting to what God will do with us when He takes hold of us. *He* will do all the cleaning.

An awareness that God is the author and finisher of our faith, that He is the One who accomplishes all the work of saving and sanctifying, that He is the One who preserves us to the end, results necessarily in humility.

Anne thought of her Christian life in this way. She was preeminently a holy woman of God, but she did not identify herself in this way. "I am confounded to think that God, who hath done so much for me, should have so little from me."[109]

This is one of the curiosities of sanctification. The more someone progresses in the faith, the more they realize how far they have to go. When the apostle Paul first repented, his repentance was genuine—he knew that he was a sinner. Ananias told him to come to baptism understanding that he had to wash his sins away. But many years later, after much faithful service, Paul identified himself as the chief of sinners.

The more we grow in grace, the more we understand how great grace is and how much it covers. Anne

Bradstreet's understanding of herself in this regard was typical of a faithful Puritan. Because she had a strong doctrinal view of human depravity, she came also to a high view of grace.

She would have had no use for "high self-esteem" as a goal for understanding herself. The flesh has more than enough of *that*, and it must be subdued and mortified. Knowing how much God has done is the key to understanding what He is doing in the present and how much He will do in the future. And that, as Anne Bradstreet knew, was the key to holiness.

CONTENTMENT

*T*HE APOSTLE PAUL said that he had learned the secret of being content, whether well fed or hungry. It is a difficult lesson to learn. When someone has learned it, it is easy for others who have not to assume that the contented individual is a stoic or a block of wood.

But contentment is not a stiff-upper-lip stoicism. All the pressures to discontent are felt, but they are not allowed to overwhelm. One area where Anne had to learn contentment was in the absences of her dear husband. In one poem, written after her husband was gone, she referred to my "dumpish thoughts, my groans, my brakish tears."[110]

Dumpish thoughts—they are the antithesis of contentment. But she then offers up all her sighs to the One who knows the number of leaves in the forest.

She also had to work through all the issues of contentment when the Bradstreet house, with all her precious possessions inside, burned to the ground. As she lamented the loss, she then turned to God, as the psalmist did so many times:

> *Then straight I 'gin my heart to chide*
> *And did thy wealth on earth abide?*
> *Didst fix thy hope on mod'ring dust?*
> *The arm of flesh didst make thy trust?*
> *Raise up thy thoughts above the sky*
> *That dunghill mists away may fly.*[111]

Anne Bradstreet loved what God had given her here, but she knew her faith better than to think her present possessions were her final inheritance.

> *The world no longer let me love,*
> *My hope and treasure lie above.*[112]

But there is no doubt that the most difficult thing for her was learning godly contentment in the deaths of grandchildren. This was not altered by the fact that children dying in that time was common. The parents and grandparents who lost children were not less tender because of infant and child mortality, they were simply more grieved.

Anne's granddaughter Elizabeth Bradstreet died when she was a year and a half old.

> *Blest babe, why should I once bewail thy fate,*
> *Or sigh thy days so soon were terminate,*
> *Sith thou art settled in an everlasting state.*[113]

In the midst of the trial, Anne looked to the only place we can look for comfort. If God is not completely in control, and if He is not going to bring everything to a right and joyous and eternal conclusion, then we of all men are most to be pitied.

Her granddaughter, also named Anne Bradstreet, died when she was almost four.

> *How oft with disappointment have I met,*
> *When I on fading things my hopes have set . . .*
> *More fool then I to look on that was lent*
> *As if mine own, when thus impermanent.* [114]

Her grandson, Simon Bradstreet, died when he was only a month old.

> *Three flowers, two scarcely blown, the last i' th' bud,*
> *Cropt by th' Almighty's hand; yet is He good . . .*
> *Go pretty babe, go rest with sisters twain;*
> *Among the blest in endless joys remain.* [115]

A crowning blow was the loss of her daughter-in-law, Mercy Bradstreet, who died in childbirth at the age of twenty-eight.

> *That thou, dear son, hath lost both tree and fruit . . .*
> *Cheer up, dear son, thy fainting bleeding heart,*
> *In Him alone that caused all this smart;*
> *What though thy strokes full sad and grievous be,*
> *He knows it is the best for thee and me.* [116]

For those without faith, this kind of response seems to be mere wishful thinking—God must bring it right in the end. But the resurrection of the dead is one of the central themes in Scripture. Without it, we are without biblical hope. The only alternatives to such hope are bitterness or a self-defensive refusal to love. But Anne was not bitter, and she loved deeply. She knew her Lord well. "He hath no benefit by my adversity, nor is He the better for my prosperity, but He doth it for my advantage, and that I may be a gainer by it."[117]

This wisdom fit every trial, including the times when Anne Bradstreet was herself ill. "And if he knowes that weaknes and a frail body is the best to make me a vessel fitt for his use, why should I not bare it, not only willingly but joyfully?"[118]

BALANCED

*I*N THIS imbalanced world, a balanced individual will often find himself saying, "Well, yes and no." In Christian circles, when there is a reaction away from ungodly compromise, there is a tendency to reduce every issue to a few simplistic formulas or doctrines. The next step is to approve of everyone who is with you all the way, and disapprove of everyone who shows the slightest concern about anything contained in the formula.

Anne Bradstreet was always concerned to maintain a biblical balance. This meant it was important to affirm what the Bible affirms and deny what the Bible denies. This wise subtlety is unfortunately too uncommon.

> *God doth many times both reward and punish for one and the same action, as we see in Jehu; he is rewarded with a kingdom to the fourth generation*

> *for taking vengeance on the house of Ahab; and*
> *"Yet a little while," saith God, "and I will avenge the*
> *blood of Jezreel upon the house of Jehu." He was*
> *rewarded for the matter, and yet punished for the*
> *manner, which should warn him that doth any spe-*
> *cial service for God to fix his eye on the command*
> *and not on his own ends, lest he meet with Jehu's*
> *reward, which will end in punishment.*[119]

She knew that it was not enough to do what God wanted to have done. Nor was it enough to have good motives while doing the wrong thing. That which God requires had to be done the way He required it, in the manner He required, and with the motives He required. Anything less was out of balance.

And while it was important to judge profession of faith by fruit, it was equally important to remember that individual Christians produce fruit in different ways, and under differing conditions. Christians are not compared to godliness factories, with the "product" always having to be interchangeable.

> *Christians that are so frequent in good duties that*
> *many times, the weight thereof impairs both their*
> *bodies and estates, and there are some (and they sin-*
> *cere ones, too) who have not attained to that fruitful-*
> *ness, although they aim at perfection, and again there*
> *are others that have nothing to commend them but*
> *only a gay profession, and these are but leavie Chris-*
> *tians which are in as much danger of being cut down*
> *as the dry stock, for both cumber the ground.*[120]

Some produce less fruit because they are less fruitful. But others do not achieve the same result, and yet they aim at perfection just like the others. God has built predictability into the world—every covenant comes with blessings and curses. We are encouraged to look at how we fare in order to understand whether we are living under the blessing of God. At the same time, our analysis of such things must not be *wooden*. We must be balanced and not veer off into extremes.

The Bradstreets held to what might be called a principled moderation. They were not given to extremes nor did they give way to simplistic analysis. Their moderation was principled because it had the force of conviction—they were willing to discipline in terms of it.

Understanding this balance helps us understand the situations with Roger Williams and Anne Hutchinson. The imbalance, the impatience shown in those situations were shown by Williams and Hutchinson. The person who has to see every reform implemented *now*, and for whom every delay is compromise, is someone who is out of balance.

There is a vast difference between the reformational mind-set and the revolutionary mind. The revolutionary wants to make a clean sweep, and he wants it now. The reformer wants to change the status quo but is willing for the leaven to work its way through the loaf. The Puritans were called Puritans because they wanted to work patiently to reform, or purify, the Church of England. Those who had given up, and who had separated themselves (as the Plymouth Plantation had done), were more vulnerable to revolutionary temptations and sentiments. But even they, it must be said, found Roger Williams to be too much.

Because the modern world is built on revolutionary assumptions, we find a natural sympathy with revolutionaries in the past, such as Roger Williams. And so when we discover that a moderate community exiled a firebrand, we tend to condemn that community for its "lack of tolerance." And, of course, they were intolerant—of impulsive and unbalanced intolerance.

So how can we measure which side had the true spirit of moderation, meekness, and balance? The answer should be plain. *Look to the individuals.* In Massachusetts, Anne Bradstreet represented the mind of balanced sanity well.

SACRIFICIAL

ANNE BRADSTREET followed the injunction of Scripture, which calls upon Christians to be prepared to give themselves away for one another. She was a sacrificial woman.

One of the things that distressed her about her illnesses was the fact that they interfered with her ability to do this. She was therefore grateful when God granted healing—"yet hath my God given me many a respite and some ability to perform the duties I owe to Him and the work of my family."[121] She wanted to be able to give herself away, and when illness prevented it, she was unhappy that the sickness was robbing her family of her ability to serve them.

But her sacrifices also took an unusual turn. "Among the few English women writers before her none displayed so encyclopedic a mind."[122] As careful students can testify, having an encyclopedic mind does not come about through wishing for one. It comes about as the result of hard work and study.

John Woodbridge noted that Anne's poetry was written in hours snatched away from sleep. We may assume that her other literary pursuits, her studies which gave her grist for the mill, were conducted the same way. In other words, Anne was not reading and studying instead of caring for her family. She did not have her nose in a book when children needed to be fed and cared for.

Now this was a sacrifice she sought out and pursued. No one required this of her, and she had more than enough to do in her ordinary responsibilities. But apparently, the creative impulses in her were very strong and demanded an outlet. But there was no way to create this outlet without tremendous late-night sacrifices. The fruit of those sacrifices are still with us today.

There were also sacrifices imposed on her by the authority of God. She was sacrificial in her demeanor here as well, and this is yet another point where modern critics badly misunderstand her. One instance of this misunderstanding was a poem written after the death of one of her grandchildren. Kenneth Murdock comments on some of the lines in the poem:

> And two lines begin to flicker toward passionate rebellion: "But plants new set to be eradicate, / And buds new blown to have so short a date"—but for the Puritan that way danger lay, and Anne Bradstreet, in deference to her creed, checks herself

> *with the inept last line "Is by his hand alone that guides nature and fate."* [123]

For Murdock, true poetry was found in her incipient rebellion against the God of the Bible, and that dry old orthodoxy brought her down to the ground with a thud. Passionate rebellion is something our generation understands, but quiet acquiescence to the will of God is beyond us—especially when it involves a divine appointment of a sacrifice we must make.

We live in a world where sacrifices will be made. We will all die, and before that happens it is likely that people dear to us will die. The sacrifice is a given, and reality is not really optional.

In this kind of situation, the sacrificial heart is that which accepts what the hand of God has delivered. Those who reject it must still deal with the *fact* of the sacrifice. Their rejection of God's determinations is simply a fast way of becoming bitter. The only sane response is to glorify God and willingly accept the sacrifices He has assigned.

This, of course, is contrary to every fleshly impulse. It is contrary to the fleshly impulses of those who are well-disciplined in the ways of God. Anne Bradstreet openly declares when the sacrifice is hard. In this, she is not rebelling against the God of the Bible. In fact, the God of the Bible, in the incarnation and death of Jesus Christ, did exactly the same thing. He cried out on the cross, in the midst of the greatest sacrifice ever made, "My God, my God, why have You forsaken Me?" This was not the beginning of a passionate rebellion but rather an essential part of the greatest submission that ever occurred.

When Christians imitate their Lord in the midst of their lesser sacrifices, the same pattern occurs. King David said that he would not sacrifice to the Lord that which cost him nothing. These lesser sacrifices follow the example of the Garden—this is not what I want. Have this cup pass from me. But if it is what You want, then my prayer is that Your will would be done.

This is the meaning of true sacrifice.

THANKFUL

*O*NE OF the great sins in the Bible is a refusal to give thanks to God for His great mercies to us. In the first chapter of Romans, Paul describes those who refuse to honor God as God and who refuse to give Him thanks. Such individuals come to a wretched end and wind up worshipping the creature rather than the Creator.

In opposition to this refusal to give thanks is the responsibility that we have to give thanks constantly for all things. For example, Paul says—"Giving thanks always for all things unto God and the Father in the name of our Lord Jesus Christ (Eph. 5:20)." The grace of thanksgiving is to be in evidence all the time. It is to be shown for all things. It is to be offered up in the name of the Lord Jesus Christ.

When Simon came back from his embassy to England, Anne wrote a poem of "almost inarticulate exclamation of thanks and praise."[124] She was not just happy he was home; she was extraordinarily thankful:

> *Thy mercies, Lord, have been so great*
> *In number numberless,*
> *Impossible for to recount*
> *Or any way express.*[125]

But it is important to note that Anne's thanksgiving is functioning here the way all Christian thanks should function. We cannot begin to thank God for all His mercies toward us. We are unaware of the vast majority of them—for instance, your liver at this moment is doing a number of things to keep you alive. Each of us, every day, is standing under a Niagara of blessings, and when we "give thanks" it is as though we have taken a small teaspoon and ladled out some of the water and given thanks to God for that.

We cannot begin to thank God for everything. But at least we can recognize and confess our inability. This is what Anne is doing in the poem cited above. Just as giving a tithe at church is giving 10 percent as a tangible indicator that God owns it *all*, and just as resting on the Lord's Day shows that every day is His, in the same way, appropriate rendering of thanks is representative. That is, we offer thanksgiving in various areas as ways of expressing our gratitude for all the things we cannot begin to number.

As she recognizes that there is no way to express thanks for all His blessings, in a mysterious way, this kind of prayer expresses that thanks.

She knew she had much to be thankful for. She came from a wonderful family. She had a loving husband. Her children were healthy and grew up to be productive citizens. And as we consider this, it would be easy to say (as Satan did in the book of Job), does Anne Bradstreet serve God for nothing?

And so when she found her family touched by tragedy, when grandchildren died, she responded in the same godly way. She displayed a thankful heart. The God who gave such wonderful gifts can never change, and so the duty of thanksgiving does not change.

There is a great deal of wisdom in thanksgiving. Paul tells us, "Be anxious for nothing, but in everything by prayer and supplication, with thanksgiving, let your requests be made known to God; and the peace of God, which surpasses all understanding, will guard your hearts and minds through Christ Jesus (Phil. 4:6–7)." We tend to want our hearts and minds to protect the peace of God within us. Paul actually reverses this and says that the peace of God protects our hearts and minds. But this does not happen simply because we present our petitions to God. It is quite possible to be anxious on our knees. We might list all our concerns and have it be nothing but a worry session in prayer. Paul says, in effect, that the thing necessary to keep this from happening is thanksgiving. We must present our petitions *with thanksgiving.*

Because the Puritans had a strong doctrine of God's providence, they saw the hand of the Lord in everything. A difficulty was reason to ask if God was chastising. A blessing was cause for great rejoicing and thanksgiving. If a hard providence arose and no sin could be connected with it, then God was to be thanked, and the trial was to be endured with patience.

In this, Anne was a typical Puritan of her day. She saw her illnesses as visitations from the Lord, and she was grateful when God in His mercy brought them to an end. She saw every event, however trivial, as part of God's overall purpose and plan. Consequently, because He is good, He is always to be thanked.

For many modern Christians, this is an alien way of thinking. Bad things are brought about "by Satan," and there is therefore no immediate comfort or hope. The only basis for hope in times of trial is a strong faith in the sovereignty of God.

This is a faith which Anne Bradstreet certainly had, and which sustained her through many trials. It also broke out, on many occasions, in glad thanksgiving.

DEATH

LIKE ALL faithful Christians, Anne knew that to live was Christ and that to die was gain. G. K. Chesterton once distinguished two different mentalities that resulted in fearlessness concerning death. One does not fear death because life is contemptible and worthless. This, ultimately, is the worldview of the suicide. But the Christian view is far different. Life is Christ, and death is more Christ. Life is beloved, and death is the Beloved.

At the same time, because of sin, and because of the fallenness of the world, certain aspects of this life can make us weary, and we can groan under the weight of it.

Three years before Anne's death, she wrote a poem entitled "As Weary Pilgrim." This is the only poem she ever wrote which survives in her handwriting. Speaking of the grave, she said:

> *What though my flesh shall there consume,*
> *It is the bed Christ did perfume,*

> *And when a few years shall be gone,*
> *This mortal shall be clothed upon.*
> *A corrupt carcass down it lays,*
> *A glorious body it shall rise.* [126]

In other words, the path of discipleship, the path that follows Christ, follows Him also down to the grave. As Luther once said, death is the culmination of our baptism. When we are tempted, we remember that Christ was tempted. When we are hungry, we remember that Christ was hungry. When we come to the grave, we remember, as Anne did, that Christ has walked this path before us. His body was laid in a grave, just as ours will be. And, of course, the ultimate hope here is that of the resurrection from the dead.

We have no detailed account of her deathbed, but we know that she was quite sick in the few years preceding her death. Despite this, she "lived to be sixty, a remarkable age considering the ruggedness of the times and the weakness of her body." [127]

Her only child to die before she did was Dorothy, in 1672. Because Anne wrote no elegiac poem for her, it is probable that she was too weak to write such a poem, and it is even possible that Anne did not find out about her eldest daughter's death.

The one account that we have of how she faced death came from her son, Simon. He said this in his diary:

> *September 16. 1672. My ever honoured & most dear*
> *Mother was translated to Heaven. Her death was*
> *occasioned by a consumption being wasted to skin &*

*bone & She had an issue made in her arm bee: she
was much troubled with rheum, & one of [the]
women [that] tended herr dressing her arm, sd shee
never saw such an arm in her Life, I, sd my most dear
Mother, but [that] arm shall bee a Glorious Arm.*

*I being absent [from] her lost the opportunity of
comitting to memory her pious & memorable xpres-
sions uttered in her sicknesse. O [that] the good
Lord would give unto me and mine a heart to walk
in her steps, considering what the end of her Conversation was, [that] so wee might one day have a
happy & glorious greeting.*[128]

Anne's son Dudley was the town clerk of Andover,
and so he was possibly the one who entered the account
of her death in the Vital Records:

*Mrs An Bradstreet: wife of Mr Simon Bradstreet
dyed 16 September and was buried the Wednesday
after.*[129]

She died looking forward to the day of resurrection,
the day when soul and body would once again be reunited.

*Then soule and body shall unite
and of their maker have the sight
Such lasting ioyes, shall there behold
as eare ner' heard nor tongue e'er told
Lord make me ready for that day
then Come deare bridgrome Come away.*[130]

The poem is not punctuated with her usual care, and indicates, perhaps, that she was too weak or ill to go over the poem as carefully as she usually did.

No stone or marker indicates where she is buried. That will be revealed, as she well knew, on the Last Day.

SIGNIFICANCE

*A*NNE BRADSTREET'S poetry has been nothing if not persistent. "The second edition, revised from the first, appeared in 1678; a third, actually a reprinting of the second, in 1758; the scholarly edition of John Harvard Ellis in 1867; an edition edited by Charles Eliot Norton, one of her descendants, in 1897; and two reprints of the Ellis edition by Peter Smith in 1932 and 1962."[131]

In addition, all the indications are that as long as English poetry is anthologized (which should be for a while yet), Anne Bradstreet's work will have an ongoing presence there.

Cotton Mather aptly called her poetry "a Monument for her Memory beyond the Statliest Marbles." A generation later, Edward Taylor, a very significant New England poet and minister, had only one book of poetry in his library, and that was Anne Bradstreet's.[132] His gifts in the poetic realm have been widely recognized, and the fact that he kept Anne's poetry in his library (and no others) is significant.

In 1675, Milton's nephew Edward Phillips in his *Theatrum Poetarum* "gave her brief but complimentary notice."[133] And as the years and centuries have passed, the critical opinion of her work has risen steadily—despite patronizing comments here and there. We must "now affirm that our first poet was a genuine, if minor, poet."[134]

Her accomplishment in this was notable, and it was a first. "No woman writing in English before Anne Bradstreet was able to create a body of verse that has been remembered with so much respect."[135] She was the greatest American poetess before Emily Dickinson, and, unlike Dickinson, she did this while living a full and rich life. In large part, this was because Anne was settled in her faith, while Emily Dickinson was anything but settled. And this, I believe, points to Anne Bradstreet's true significance, which is the fact that she was Puritan woman. This is not a historical accident or fluke. Her poetry arose out of her faith, was entirely consistent with it, and indeed was created by it. Her contribution could not have been made in any other setting.

Appreciating the significance of Anne Bradstreet therefore means appreciating the significance of the Puritans. Moreover, this appreciation must not be of the grudging variety that is sometimes given to them. "Yes, the Puritans were a hardy and courageous people, and they were God's grouches, but nevertheless, despite their hard edges, we do owe them something."

No, appreciating their legacy means learning to recognize how they did *well* in areas where everyone believes them to have done poorly. Anne Bradstreet represents the Puritans at their best, and she was not a lonely, isolated representative. She lived in a day when her contribution was respected and honored by many in her community. We must not consider Puritanism in decline, or at its worst, and then say that Anne Bradstreet was a mysterious exception to the prevailing harshness. She was rather a loved and respected woman in her family and in her community. She was held up as an ideal for the broader community. All this was done for a reason.

In many places throughout this book, this has been said in so many words: "The Puritans are commonly thought to have been this way, but they actually were not. They were actually the opposite of this." As long as Anne Bradstreet continues to win respect, and as long as the Puritans continue to be slandered, it will be necessary to make this point again and again. Even the most thorough and best detailed biography of Anne Bradstreet stumbles at this point. Elizabeth White says:

> *It is as a human being, however, that she can still appeal to us over the centuries. She had a firm and lively character, avid for knowledge, generous in affection and admiration, with a quiet but perceptive humor and a philosophy that was able to transcend, in its humanistic tolerance and wisdom, the rigid conformity of the Calvinistic thought-patterns of her community.*

"She was a nice lady." Too bad about all her friends and family, and everything she loved and held dear.

This error goes beyond the obvious problems of association and ignores how *dependent* she was on her culture. She did not derive her inspiration as a rebellious romantic poet, writing poetic cries of anguish against the Establishment. The founder of American literature loved and wrote from within a community.

And so this is her significance. When believing Christians today are told that faith in the God of the Bible is inconsistent with having "poetic soul," there are many places they can point—and one of them is the life of Anne Bradstreet. When modern Christian women are told that submitting to and honoring a husband destroys a woman's identity, they can point to a woman whose life makes the opposite point. And when they are told that the artist must be a solitary loner, they can shake their heads and mention the woman who wrote poetry in the middle of the parish.

PART 3
THE LEGACY OF
ANNE BRADSTREET

NOBILITY

ONE OF the lessons of Anne Bradstreet's life, an important part of her legacy, arises from her nobility. This does not refer to the word in the way it would be used in our modern democratic setting. We tell every child that he or she could eventually become president of the United States. On paper, this is quite true, if we are considering nothing but constitutional qualifications. But when we consider abilities and genuine opportunities, it becomes obvious that we are lying.

In the days of Queen Elizabeth, the son of a stable-hand was never told that he might grow up to be the king.

Society at that time was overtly hierarchical. There was an aristocracy on one end and the common people on the other. These were not the only two categories—a rising merchant class was setting the stage for coming social upheavals, and, of course, there were a number of families that were educated and genteel with connections to aristocracy. Anne Dudley was born into a family in this last category.

Society at that time was *overtly* hierarchical. Ours is just as hierarchical, but out of deference to democratic platitudes, we pretend that it isn't. This doesn't make our ruling class disappear, but it does make it easier for them to manipulate us. In the older system, there was a ruling class, but the Christian standard of *noblesse oblige* was imposed upon it. To whom much is given, much is required.

"When Thomas Dudley, as an old man in Massachusetts, wrote his will in 1653, he affixed to it a seal bearing a lion rampant with single tail and with a crescent for difference, that is, to show descent from a younger son of the baronial house."[1] The elder Dudley knew his ancestry and "his own children and descendants left some indications that they shared this knowledge."[2]

In Anne Bradstreet's elegy to Sir Philip Sidney, she says something that perhaps indicates her awareness, not only of her relation to Sidney, but also of her aristocratic lineage.

> *Let then, none dis-allow of these my straines,*
> *Which have the self-same blood yet in my veines.*[3]

Out of an apparent concern over vainglory, she amended these lines for any subsequent editions of her poetry. But their initial insertion shows her awareness of not having been basely born. And with that awareness, and this is the whole point, came a world of assumptions about the need to exercise responsibility, leadership, setting a good example, and so forth.

We know for certain who Thomas Dudley's father was, but his grandfather is not named by the family. But all the indications are that this grandfather was named George Dudley, and his wild career helps to indicate why his family didn't have his picture hanging over the mantel.

"And if Thomas, Roger's son, was descended from the soldier of fortune George Dudley, conspirataor against at least two of his country's monarchs, expedient Knight of Malta, turncoat in religion and deserter of his wife, it would surely account for the reluctance of the righteous old governor of Massachusetts to make public the facts of his grandfather's life."[4]

George Dudley was the aristocratic equivalent of a horse thief in the family tree, but nevertheless he was in fact an *aristocratic* horse thief.

With this background, the rude manners of colonial life were quite a trial. Anne Bradstreet "and her father both referred sadly to the 'manners' that the pioneering life engendered."[5]

This concern over manners was not an example of tender people not being able to adjust to rough conditions. The concern over manners was a desire to see civilization planted in New England. Not only was this the case, but the Puritans saw this emphasis on manners as being more than a matter of tradition. His religion called for this. "But the Puritan's code of good manners was an integral part of his standard of Christian conduct, and for these devout colonists, especially those among them who had been privileged to live gently in England, it must have been disheartening to see . . . [manners] fail under the weight of outrageous circumstance."[6]

The Puritans wanted to establish Christian civilization on the coasts of America. But they knew that this could not be done without a nobility setting an example for all the people. And despite the rude manners and customs that life in the early colony encouraged, the Puritans succeeded in establishing the essential features of the older order of Christendom on these shores. That order was eventually to perish in the early nineteenth century, but the destructive forces at work in this were also at work, and in a worse way, in the old world.

Anne Bradstreet saw herself as a privileged woman, as part of a new *ad hoc* nobility. This new nobility was started from a remnant of the older order, but was genuinely part of it. But in the best traditions of aristocracy, this was manifested in humility and grace, and not in a haughty spirit that has sometimes made aristocracy offensive.

Her legacy in this regard should lead us to question some of our democratic assumptions, which are clearly at war with the Christian faith.

POETRY

*O*F COURSE, Anne Bradstreet was a gifted poet. But her legacy for us in this respect is particularly important. "And her destiny held two gifts of more worth than worldly riches, a happy and fruitful marriage, and the power to translate her thoughts into verse that was acclaimed in her own time and that is still, three hundred years after her life's end, read with respect and pleasure."[7]

Her poetry does bring great pleasure. And she wrote her poetry in the midst of a believing community that encouraged her in the writing of it. "New England Puritans constantly read poetry—or at least verse—and hundreds of them tried their hands at writing it . . . It is safe to say that the New England Puritans, far from being hostile to poetry, both needed and loved it."[8]

So her legacy at this point has two important aspects. The first is simply the quality of her best poetry.

She was good. "Anne Bradstreet, the first American poetess and one whose work is more imaginative and more skillful in its use of some Renaissance techniques than that of any other New England Puritan except Edward Taylor . . ."[9] It is important for us to honor her achievement as a poet, and that has been the goal of this book throughout.

But a legacy by definition brings lessons with it. The lesson for us here is a severe one. In our modern world, the more conservative in theology a particular church or denomination is, the *less* likely they are to love poetry. Many conservative believers and defenders of the faith have sought to do their work through doctrinal engineering and theological abstractions. This has resulted in a truncated form of the faith—which is what the faith looks like whenever it compromises with the forces of modernity. Far from providing an alternative to modernity, this kind of Christianity is simply the "conservative" capitulation to modernity.

Of course, on the other extreme is that wing of the Church that does not care about theology or orthodoxy at all, but rather wants to bask in the warm glow of sentiment. But in order to provoke a sentimental response, bad poetry will do quite nicely. People rhyme *moon* with *June* for a reason. Somebody likes it.

So we have, on the one hand, conservative (but simultaneously modern) believers who have no soul, or at least souls with no room for poetry. On the other hand, we have gushy souls into which the contents of every Mother's Day card ever written have been poured.

We must do better than this. Christians who believe the Bible must recover an understanding of the importance of poetry—*good* poetry. The Word of God, which God *gave* to us, contains vast stretches of glorious poetry. But we tend to treat it as a grab bag for doctrinal prooftexts or inspirational quotes. But in reading the Word of God rightly, we rediscover what might be called the romance of orthodoxy.

In other eras, when Christians read their Bibles as they ought to have, and when they approached God in worship the way He requires, the result has consistently been an outbreak of poetic thinking, poetic knowledge, and poetic worship. It is our era, compromised as it has been with the forces of modernity, which is so poverty-stricken in this respect.

Few Christians today realize that the history of poetry in English is overwhelmingly the history of *Christian* poetry.[10] This is our legacy, our treasure house, which we have grossly neglected. Anne Bradstreet's work is very much part of this stream, but we in the modern era of the faith have sought in our ignorance to dam the stream.

We have to recover the older standards for writing poetry, and if we have the slightest inclination, we should encourage it as much as we can. Good books are available to help us in this.[11] The first stuff we write will probably not be very good, but we should laugh at it and keep going. We are laboring for the kingdom.

In addition to learning the mechanics of writing poetry, we should thoroughly acquaint ourselves with the best poetry that has been written. We should begin reading through anthologies and collections. As we work our way through anthologies, we will be pleased to run across our friend Anne Bradstreet. We will also be pleased to note how well her poetry compares with what came before her and with what came after.

If we are homeschooling, or if we are associated with Christian schools, we will reinstitute the memorization of poetry in the curriculum. Not only will we reinstitute memorization, but we will reinstitute memorization of vast amounts. It is a shame that several generations ago even the government schools required more poetic memorization than do many Christian schools today.

What we are looking for is a reformation and a renaissance. We are not looking for a "movement." We are looking forward to the day when a Christian who wants to "make a difference" will not think first of running for Congress, but will rather find a pleasant place in the library and will set himself to write a poem. He might do well to dedicate it to Anne Bradstreet.

WOMANHOOD

WE LIVE in a time of great sexual confusion. In our public life, we now have heterosexuals, homosexuals, lesbians, bisexuals, and those numbered among the transgendered. No doubt work in a laboratory somewhere is trying to come up with a few more options for us.

In Anne Bradstreet's day, the roles for men and women were defined, understood, and loved. The result, naturally, was remarkable social stability. But because of our current widespread democratic egalitarianism, to call for a return to this older, simpler (and biblical) social order is no doubt a thought violation or hate crime of some sort. But it is something we must call for regardless. So please finish this chapter before calling the authorities.

The legacy of Anne Bradstreet in this regard is that she enables us to refute the slanders brought by those who hate the older social order. Those slanders keep coming because it is hard to argue with how God created the world. The debate between the forces of egalitarianism and those who embrace the biblical order is not a debate between those who want to paint something blue and those who want to paint it red. Rather it is a debate between those who want to let water run downhill and those who want to sweep it up the hill. The egalitarians have to argue for their position *constantly*, and so we find them taking every shot they can. Anne Bradstreet has left us with a wonderful collection of answers.

We are told that a biblical social order does not respect women. And so we turn to Anne, who was one of the most highly respected individuals in New England.

We are told that in a biblical society, women would not be educated. And so we look to the stern and gracious Thomas Dudley, a rock-ribbed Puritan if ever there was one, who saw to it that his daughter was one of the best-educated individuals in the colony.

We are told that women in a biblical society would be sexually repressed. And so, again, we turn to Anne Bradstreet, who was passionately devoted to her husband and not at all ashamed of it.

We are told that women must have access to the world of corporate advancement in order to find fulfillment in their lives. And so we turn to Anne Bradstreet who gave herself away to her family, complete and fulfilled.

We are told that women are oppressed through having to bear children, and if they must bear any, it ought to be around 1.2 children. Anne Bradstreet had eight little ones, all of whom delighted her. They were not a burden for her soul—they were her soul's refreshment and joy.

We are told that a biblical treatment of women will result in them having to live up on a china doll pedestal. So again we look to find Anne Bradstreet laboring faithfully for her household in the wilderness.

Not only does Anne provide us with a counter-example for virtually every slander, we find that the accusations made against her (and her sisters), all shown to be false, remind us of something. The accusations can be turned around.

Does our secular culture respect women? Pretends to. But vicious attacks on women are commonplace in the pop music of our day. "Respect for women" is demanded if the target is sexually segregated submarines. The powers-that-be want to station women on submarines because it is too hard to molest them when we leave them on shore. Our intellectualoids' true intent is seen in how they respond when some rap "artist" wants to rape and dismember women. Our feminist culture today hates women, despises them.

Education? Our current establishment doesn't know how to educate anyone, including the girls.

When it comes to sexual repression, we find as much sexual unhappiness in our society today (among women) as has ever existed. Women today typically have to deal with the baggage caused by a series of failed relationships. The sexual revolution was a revolution of promiscuous males, for promiscuous males, and by promiscuous males. The women who were manipulated into going along with it (and there were many) did not have a fraction of the sexual contentment experienced by women such as Anne Bradstreet.

As for success in the corporate world, women have been told here that in order to be fulfilled they have to be like men. They have to want what men want, they have to compete the way men compete, they have to deny themselves—and not in the way Jesus said we have to deny ourselves. They must deny how God made them, which means denying their essential femininity. Some of them manage it, but the results are not pretty.

Barrenness is not something that can satisfy a woman. If the loss is God-given, then a godly woman can find her satisfaction in His will. But when it is self-induced, the dissatisfaction is profound. And this is something that even many feminists have lately discovered, as they have begun listening to their "biological clocks."

It is quite false that Puritan women were porcelain doll figures. They were women, created in the image of God, designed by Him to complement the men. But if we flip this around, we do find that young girls today *are* encouraged to become Barbie dolls. And so they do, growing up to acquire their big breasts, just like Barbie, and usually made out of the same kind of material.

For young girls today, it should be quite clear that Anne Bradstreet provides a godly model of biblical womanhood.

COMMUNITY

*A*NOTHER IMPORTANT part of Anne's legacy can be seen in the fact that she lived her life and made her contribution as a member of a believing community. Not only was it a believing community, it was a thoughtful, educated community. "The New England Puritans had brains, education, and culture."[12]

Because it was a community, it was possible to draw on the strength of shared convictions. Because it was a believing community, those shared convictions had the advantage of being, well, true. And because it was an educated community, it was not a group of people who had accidentally stumbled upon the truth. As believers they knew what they believed, and as educated believers, they knew why.

Contrary to the myths of individualism, God has created us to live in community together. At the center of every believing community is the worship of God in His Church. But in the modern world, our cohesiveness has been lost because we have forgotten the centrality of the Church in the world. We were put into the world to be the salt of it. Christ has established a light in the Church that is to be the light of the world. And in a very famous quotation (in New England) of a well-known passage of the Bible, the believing community is designed to be a city on hill, to be seen by all.

Most churches today are not at the center of anything that could be called a community, or parish. They are not a city on a hill but rather a chapel in the valley. Or, increasingly, we see some churches trying to become a mall in the suburbs. They are religious clubs, which sometimes degenerate into social clubs, but they are not the thriving center of a thriving township or community.

Worship is to be the center of our lives, and if our worship is right, grounded in the Word of God, then the center of our lives is right. Urban sprawl, suburban sprawl, strip-mall creep, all present a great challenge to the modern church. As we consider the challenges, and as we study our Bibles in a search for answers, a helpful occasional response will be to turn to read about those times when the community spread out from the Church, and the Church was what it was designed by God to be. Reading about such times can bring great soul refreshment.

Anne Bradstreet's legacy in this regard is that she did not do anything by herself. She did not roam off by herself into the woods of America, a solitary figure, writing in a lonely voice. She wrote as a *member.* She was connected and understood those connections. She loved and was beloved. The debt we owe to her (and it is considerable), we owe also in part to everyone who loved her and who was loved in return.

Another poet showed us that no man is an island. We are designed by God to be dependent upon one another, to need one another. We are not detachable, interchangeable carbon units. We are not meatware. Anne wrote with these connections in mind, and if we read her without some understanding of these community connections, we will radically misread her.

This has been one of the protests throughout this book. Modern critics consistently try to separate her from her community, her Calvinism, her politics, her children, and her commitments. It cannot work. The only way she could be separated in any way from her commitments and connections in seventeenth-century New England was through her death. And even in death, she immediately found herself in the midst of larger, greater, heavenly connections, of which her believing earthly community was a lovely part.

In closing our study of Anne Bradstreet, a point that needs to be emphasized again is that our era has much to learn from the *community* of Puritans who first settled in New England. And we cannot learn what we need to if we keep slandering them. We must take stock of our situation and consider our condition. Joseph Lee, in a letter to the *Boston Herald*, isolated the poverty of our modern arguments this way.

> *The case against the Puritans is conclusive. We of the present generation have two kinds of faults;*

puritanical and otherwise—especially otherwise.
The former are clearly a direct inheritance from the
Puritans, the latter a reaction against them. Both
kinds are thus the faults of the Puritans and of no
one else. We ourselves, accordingly, have no faults.
This is what we have always felt, but it has never
been so clearly proved before. [13]

We have a clear responsibility to understand and appreciate Anne Bradstreet. And we cannot understand or appreciate her without coming to understand the Puritans. This is because she was an educated, gracious, lovely *Puritan* woman—and someday we will learn that this is not oxymoronic.

Notes

Part 1: The Life of Anne Bradstreet

1. For those open to understanding the Puritans as they really were, the place to start is with Leland Ryken, *The Worldly Saints* (Grand Rapids, MI: Zondervan, 1986).
2. Josephine Piercy, *Anne Bradstreet* (New York: Twayne Publishers, Inc., 1965), 22.
3. Kenneth Murdock, *Literature and Theology in Colonial New England* (Westport, CT: Greenwood Press, 1949), 151.
4. George Dow, *Every Day Life in the Massachusetts Bay Colony* (New York: Dover Publications, Inc., 1988), 108.
5. Ibid., 114.
6. Anne Bradstreet, *The Works of Anne Bradstreet*, Jeannine Hensley, ed. (Cambridge, Mass.: Harvard University Press, 1967), 70.
7. Ibid., 72.
8. George Dow, *Every Day Life in the Massachusetts Bay Colony*, 45.
9. Josephine Piercy, *Anne Bradstreet*, 22.
10. George Dow, *Every Day Life in the Massachusetts Bay Colony*, 200.
11. Samuel Morison, *Builders of the Bay Colony* (New York: Houghton Mifflin, 1930), 218.
12. Ibid., 219.
13. Josephine Piercy, *Anne Bradstreet*, 111.

14. Anne Bradstreet, *The Works of Anne Bradstreet*, Jeannine Hensley, ed., xxv. Emphasis mine.
15. Ibid., xxi.
16. Ibid., xxvii.
17. Ibid., 16.
18. Ibid.
19. Ibid., 196.
20. Ibid., 198.
21. Ibid., 240–41.
22. Ibid., 241.
23. Ibid.
24. Ibid.
25. Cotton Mather, *The Great Works of Christ in America* (Carlisle, PA: Banner of Truth Trust, 1979 [1702]), 138–40.
26. Anne Bradstreet, *The Works of Anne Bradstreet*, Jeannine Hensley, ed., 225. Incidentally, it should be noted that Anne pronounced "persevere" differently than do we.
27. Ibid., xxv.
28. Ibid., 224.
29. Ibid., 226.
30. Ibid., 229.
31. C. S. Lewis, *English Literature in the Sixteenth Century*, (Oxford: Oxford University Press, 1954), 35.
32. Leland Ryken, *Worldly Saints*, 39–54.
33. Alan Heimert & Andrew Delbanco, *The Puritans in America* (Cambridge, Mass.: Harvard University Press, 1985), 75–76.
34. George Dow, *Every Day Life in the Massachusetts Bay Colony*, 9.
35. Josephine Piercy, *Anne Bradstreet*, 18.
36. Elizabeth Wade White, *Anne Bradstreet: The Tenth Muse* (New York: Oxford University Press, 1971), 104.
37. George Dow, *Every Day Life in the Massachusetts Bay Colony*, 8.
38. Ibid., 8–9.
39. Elizabeth Wade White, *Anne Bradstreet: The Tenth Muse*, 109.
40. George Dow, *Every Day Life in the Massachusetts Bay Colony*, 106.
41. Ibid., 17.

42. Ibid., 16.
43. Ibid., 19.
44. Ibid., 39–40.
45. Ibid., 41.
46. Ibid., 85.
47. Ibid., 129.
48. Ibid., 41.
49. Ibid., 149.
50. Ibid., 150.
51. Anne Bradstreet, *The Works of Anne Bradstreet*, Jeannine Hensley, ed., ix.
52. Ibid.
53. George Dow, *Every Day Life in the Massachusetts Bay Colony*, 178.
54. Ibid., 185.
55. Ibid., 219.
56. Josephine Piercy, *Anne Bradstreet*, 24.
57. Cotton Mather, *The Great Works of Christ in America*, 133.
58. Elizabeth Wade White, *Anne Bradstreet: The Tenth Muse*, 3–41.
59. George Dow, *Every Day Life in the Massachusetts Bay Colony*, 19.
60. Cotton Mather, *The Great Works of Christ in America*, 134.
61. Anne Bradstreet, *The Works of Anne Bradstreet*, Jeannine Hensley, ed., 231.
62. Cotton Mather, *The Great Works of Christ in America*, 134–35.
63. For an example of this kind of sympathy hunt, see Josephine Piercy, *Anne Bradstreet*, 28.
64. Anne Bradstreet, *The Works of Anne Bradstreet*, Jeannine Hensley, ed., 14.
65. Ibid., 201.
66. Ibid.
67. Ibid., 202.
68. Ibid., 203.
69. Ibid., xi.
70. Ibid., 14.
71. Ibid., xii–xiii.
72. Ibid., xiii.

73. Ibid., 29.
74. Josephine Piercy, *Anne Bradstreet*, 59ff.
75. Anne Bradstreet, *The Works of Anne Bradstreet*, Jeannine Hensley, ed., 34.
76. Ibid., 35.
77. Ibid., 48.
78. Ibid., 67.
79. Josephine Piercy, *Anne Bradstreet* (New York: Twayne Publishers, Inc., 1965), 44.
80. Edwin Gaustad, *Liberty of Conscience* (Valley Forge: Judson Press, 1999), 41.
81. Ibid., ix.
82. Anne Bradstreet, *The Works of Anne Bradstreet,* Jeannine Hensley, ed., xi.
83. Elizabeth Wade White, *Anne Bradstreet: The Tenth Muse*, 173.
84. Edwin Gaustad, *Liberty of Conscience*, 58.
85. Anne Bradstreet, *The Works of Anne Bradstreet*, Jeannine Hensley, ed., 62.
86. J. C. Ryle, *Light From Old Times* (Moscow, ID: Charles Nolan Publishers, 1999), 256–57.
87. Josephine Piercy, *Anne Bradstreet* (New York: Twayne Publishers, Inc., 1965), 77.
88. Elizabeth Wade White, *Anne Bradstreet: The Tenth Muse*, 248.
89. Anne Bradstreet, *The Works of Anne Bradstreet*, Jeannine Hensley, ed., 180.
90. Ibid., 182.
91. Anne Bradstreet, *The Works of Anne Bradstreet*, Jeannine Hensley, ed., 62.
92. Ibid., 179.
93. Josephine Piercy, *Anne Bradstreet*, 17.
94. Elizabeth Wade White, *Anne Bradstreet: The Tenth Muse*, 255.
95. Ibid.
96. Anne Bradstreet, *The Works of Anne Bradstreet*, Jeannine Hensley, ed., xv.
97. Ibid., 221.

98. Ibid., xxxi-xxxii.
99. Elizabeth Wade White, *Anne Bradstreet: The Tenth Muse*, 268.
100. Ibid., 283.
101. Ibid.
102. Ibid., 284.
103. Ibid.
104. Anne Bradstreet, *The Works of Anne Bradstreet*, Jeannine Hensley, ed., xvii.
105. Ibid., xxix.
106. Ibid., xxxi.
107. Ibid., 204.
108. Ibid., 207.
109. Ibid., 292.
110. Ibid.
111. Ibid., 271.
112. Ibid., 272.
113. Ibid., 287.
114. Ibid., 278.
115. Josephine Piercy, *Anne Bradstreet*, 33.

PART 2: THE CHARACTER OF ANNE BRADSTREET

1. Josephine Piercy, *Anne Bradstreet* (New York: Twayne Publishers, Inc., 1965), 36.
2. Ibid.
3. Anne Bradstreet, *The Works of Anne Bradstreet*, Jeannine Hensley, ed. (Cambridge, Mass.: Harvard University Press, 1967), xxvi.
4. Ibid., xxvi.
5. Ibid., 75.
6. Ibid., 172.
7. Ibid., xv.
8. Elizabeth Wade White, *Anne Bradstreet: The Tenth Muse*, (New York: Oxford University Press, 1971), 5.

9. Anne Bradstreet, *The Works of Anne Bradstreet*, Jeannine Hensley, ed., 204.

10. Elizabeth Wade White, *Anne Bradstreet: The Tenth Muse*, 90.

11. Leland Ryken, *Worldly Saints* (Grand Rapids, MI: Zondervan, 1986), 42.

12. Ibid., 47.

13. Elizabeth Wade White, *Anne Bradstreet: The Tenth Muse*, 127.

14. Ibid., 201.

15. Anne Bradstreet, *The Works of Anne Bradstreet*, Jeannine Hensley, ed., xxv.

16. George Dow, *Every Day Life in the Massachusetts Bay Colony* (New York: Dover Publications, Inc., 1988), 63.

17. Ibid., 63.

18. Ibid., 63–64.

19. Perry Miller, ed., *The American Puritans: Their Prose and Poetry*, (New York: Doubleday, 1956), 95.

20. George Dow, *Every Day Life in the Massachusetts Bay Colony* (New York: Dover Publications, Inc., 1988), 62–63.

21. Perry Miller, ed., *The American Puritans: Their Prose and Poetry*, 103.

22. Leland Ryken, *Worldly Saints*, 47.

23. Anne Bradstreet, *The Works of Anne Bradstreet*, Jeannine Hensley, ed., xi.

24. Josephine Piercy, *Anne Bradstreet* (New York: Twayne Publishers, Inc., 1965), 88.

25. Leland Ryken, *Worldly Saints*, 44.

26. Ibid., 39.

27. Ibid.

28. Ibid., 42.

29. Ibid., 46.

30. Ann Stanford, *Anne Bradstreet: The Wordly Puritan* (New York: Burt Franklin & Co, 1974), 21.

31. Anne Bradstreet, *The Works of Anne Bradstreet*, Jeannine Hensley, ed., 274.

32. Ibid., 279.

33. Ibid., 224.
34. Ibid., 232.
35. Ibid., 232.
36. This information on Anne's family came from Colonel Luther Caldwell, *An Account of Anne Bradstreet the Puritan Poetess and Kindred Topics* (Boston: Danrell & Upham, 1898), 17–18. The reader should be advised that Colonel Caldwell was something of a character.
37. Anne Bradstreet, *The Works of Anne Bradstreet,* Jeannine Hensley, ed., ix.
38. Ibid., xix.
39. Ibid.
40. Ibid., xx.
41. Ibid., xxviii.
42. Ibid., 199.
43. Ibid., 210.
44. Josephine Piercy, *Anne Bradstreet*, 99.
45. Elizabeth Wade White, *Anne Bradstreet: The Tenth Muse*, 95–96.
46. Ibid., 79.
47. Ibid., 102.
48. Ibid., 82.
49. Ibid., 214.
50. Ibid., 105.
51. Anne Bradstreet, *The Works of Anne Bradstreet*, Jeannine Hensley, ed., xvii.
52. Ibid., xvii.
53. Colonel Luther Caldwell, *An Account of Anne Bradstreet the Puritan Poetess and Kindred Topics*, 5.
54. Anne Bradstreet, *The Works of Anne Bradstreet*, Jeannine Hensley, ed., 278.
55. Ibid., 56.
56. Elizabeth Wade White, *Anne Bradstreet: The Tenth Muse*, 104.
57. Anne Bradstreet, *The Works of Anne Bradstreet*, Jeannine Hensley, ed., 258.
58. Elizabeth Wade White, *Anne Bradstreet: The Tenth Muse*, 303.

59. Ibid., 307.
60. Ibid., 305.
61. Anne Bradstreet, *The Works of Anne Bradstreet*, Jeannine Hensley, ed., 288.
62. Ibid., 281-82.
63. John Calvin, *Concerning the Eternal Predestination of God* (Cambridge, England: James Clarke & Co., 1961), 118.
64. Anne Bradstreet, *The Works of Anne Bradstreet*, Jeannine Hensley, ed., 209.
65. Ibid., 54.
66. Ibid., xi.
67. Ibid., 206.
68. Ibid., 280–81.
69. Ibid., 279.
70. Elizabeth Wade White, *Anne Bradstreet: The Tenth Muse*, 310.
71. Anne Bradstreet, *The Works of Anne Bradstreet*, Jeannine Hensley, ed.,184.
72. Ibid., 244–45.
73. Ibid., 215.
74. Ibid., 219.
75. Ibid., xiv.
76. Ibid., xiv.
77. Elizabeth Wade White, *Anne Bradstreet: The Tenth Muse*, 174.
78. Ibid., 176.
79. Ibid., 177.
80. Anne Bradstreet, *The Works of Anne Bradstreet*, Jeannine Hensley, ed., xxviii.
81. Ibid., x.
82. Elizabeth Wade White, *Anne Bradstreet: The Tenth Muse*, 128.
83. Ibid., 5–6.
84. Ibid., 220.
85. Ibid., 220.
86. Ibid., 307, 320.
87. Ibid., 302.
88. Ibid., 302.

89. Anne Bradstreet, *The Works of Anne Bradstreet,* Jeannine Hensley, ed., 275.
90. Ibid., 277.
91. Ibid., 292.
92. Ibid., 257.
93. Ibid., 186.
94. Ibid., 265.
95. Kenneth Murdock, *Literature and Theology in Colonial New England* (Westport, CT.: Greenwood Press, Publishers, 1949), 3.
96. Ibid., 2.
97. Anne Bradstreet, *The Works of Anne Bradstreet*, Jeannine Hensley, ed., 282.
98. Ibid., xxvi.
99. Ibid., 189.
100. Kenneth Murdock, *Literature and Theology in Colonial New England* (Westport, CT.: Greenwood Press, Publishers, 1949), 49.
101. Anne Bradstreet, *The Works of Anne Bradstreet*, Jeannine Hensley, ed., 285.
102. Ibid., 277.
103. Ibid., 274.
104. Ibid., 282.
105. Ibid., 277.
106. Ibid., 274.
107. Ibid., 291.
108. Ibid., 284.
109. Ibid., 250.
110. Ibid., 227.
111. Ibid., 293.
112. Ibid.
113. Ibid., 235.
114. Ibid., 236.
115. Ibid., 237.
116. Ibid., 238–39.
117. Ibid., 254.
118. Josephine Piercy, *Anne Bradstreet* (New York: Twayne Publishers, Inc., 1965), 39.

119. Anne Bradstreet, *The Works of Anne Bradstreet*, Jeannine Hensley, ed. (Cambridge, MA: Harvard University Press, 1967), 285.
120. Ibid., 287.
121. Ibid., 255.
122. Elizabeth Wade White, *Anne Bradstreet: The Tenth Muse,* 60.
123. Kenneth Murdock, *Literature & Theology in Colonial New England,* 152.
124. Elizabeth Wade White, *Anne Bradstreet: The Tenth Muse*, 321.
125. Anne Bradstreet, *The Works of Anne Bradstreet*, Jeannine Hensley, ed., 270.
126. Ibid., 295.
127. Josephine Piercy, *Anne Bradstreet*, 39.
128. Elizabeth Wade White, *Anne Bradstreet: The Tenth Muse*, 358–59.
129. Ibid., 359.
130. Ibid., 355.
131. Josephine Piercy, *Anne Bradstreet*, 114.
132. Anne Bradstreet, *The Works of Anne Bradstreet*, Jeannine Hensley, ed., xxxiii.
133. Josephine Piercy, *Anne Bradstreet*, 112–13.
134. Anne Bradstreet, *The Works of Anne Bradstreet*, Jeannine Hensley, ed., xxxvi.
135. Josephine Piercy, *Anne Bradstreet*, 116.
136. Elizabeth Wade White, *Anne Bradstreet: The Tenth Muse*, 380.

PART 3: THE LEGACY OF ANNE BRADSTREET

1. Elizabeth Wade White, *Anne Bradstreet: The Tenth Muse*, 11.
2. Ibid.
3. Ibid., 5.
4. Ibid., 29.
5. Ibid., 115.
6. Ibid., 116.
7. Ibid., 41.

8. Kenneth Murdock, *Literature & Theology in Colonial New England* (Westport, CT: Greenwood Press, 1949), 140–41.

9. Ibid., 150.

10. James H. Trott, ed., *A Sacrifice of Praise* (Nashville: Cumberland House, 1999).

11. Suzanne Clark, *The Roar on the Other Side* (Moscow, ID: Canon Press, 2000).

12. Colonel Luther Caldwell, *An Account of Anne Bradstreet* (Boston: Damrell & Upham, 1898), 39.

13. Kenneth Murdock, *Literature & Theology in Colonial New England*, 175–76.

SELECTED BIBLIOGRAPHY

Dow, George Francis, *Every Day Life in the Massachusetts Bay Colony*. New York, Dover Publications Inc., 1988.

Bradstreet, Anne, *The Works of Anne Bradstreet*, Jeannine Hensley, ed. Cambridge, Mass.: Harvard University Press, 1967.

Ryken, Leland, *The Worldly Saints*. Grand Rapids, MI: Zondervan, 1986.

White, Elizabeth Wade, *Anne Bradstreet: The Tenth Muse*. New York: Oxford University Press, 1971.

Daly, Robert, *God's Altar: The World and the Flesh in Puritan Poetry*. Berkeley, CA: University of California Press, 1978.